THE GOSPEL
FOR KIDS

Series B

ELDON WEISHEIT

Publishing House
St. Louis

Other books by Eldon Weisheit
    61 Worship Talks for Children
    61 Gospel Talks for Children
    Excuse Me, Sir
    The Zeal of His House
    The Preacher's Yellow Pants
    Moving
    To the Kid in the Pew, Series A
    To the Kid in the Pew, Series B
    To the Kid in the Pew, Series C
    The Gospel for Kids, Series A
    A Sermon Is More Than Words, Book Eight,
       The Preacher's Workshop Series

The Scripture quotations in this publication are from the Today's English Version of the New Testament. Copyright © American Bible Society 1966, 1971. Third Edition, 1973. Used by permission.

Concordia Publishing House, St. Louis, Missouri
Copyright © 1978 Concordia Publishing House
MANUFACTURED IN THE UNITED STATES OF AMERICA

Library of Congress Cataloging in Publication Data

Weisheit, Eldon.
    The Gospel for kids, series B.

    1. Children's sermons. I. Title.
BV4315.W3733   252'.5   77-29140
ISBN 0-570-03267-9

4 5 6 7 8 9 10 11 IB 89 88 87 86 85

Preface

As I was writing the last pages of the manuscript that was to become this book, I was also saying good-bye to the congregation where most of the sermons had been preached. At a farewell dinner the master of ceremonies pulled several objects from a sack—objects that were used in the sermons included in this book. Members of the congregation identified the objects by the sermons in which they were used. Soon church members were recalling other objects and challenging others to remember their applications.

Though I have long been convinced that object lessons help people remember what they hear, I was amazed at the collective memory of the congregation. Their response renewed my zeal to "see" the message of God's love in Jesus Christ as it is recorded in the Bible and to share that message in objects as well as words.

I hope that my weddings of world and word will also help you preach the full council of God. The objects and situations will have to be adjusted both to you and to your audience. Let the object be so clearly connected with the message of the word that you and your audience adjust to the way God directs you.

The messages of this book are presented as sermons for children as an addition to the Sunday morning service; the objects and ideas can be used as part of the regular sermon. Often the objects can serve as an introduction to a sermon based on the entire Gospel for the day. Or the message as given in this book may be a part addressed directly to children within the regular sermon.

May the Holy Spirit bless your preaching and teaching to others. And may the same Spirit minister to you as you minister to others.

Eldon Weisheit

3

Scripture Index

The sermons for children in this book are based on portions of the Gospels located in the three-year lectionary, Year B.

Dedicated to the teachers of Trinity Lutheran School, Roselle, Ill., 1975—77, in appreciation for the joy we shared together professionally and personally in our ministry to the children of the congregation.

Kenneth Black	Bonnie Hahn	Wendy Greve
Paul Flett	Karen Pautsch	Sharon Jensen
Erich Bredehoeft	Luann Elitt	Nancy Studt
Theo Harks	Julaine Kammrath	Candy Eichholz
Dan Homp	Pat Homp	Norma Armstrong
Terry Weslock	Naomi Weslock	Linda Harks
Evelyn Heuser	Marjorie Bredehoeft	

Contents

You Don't Know When the Phone Will Ring

The Word

Jesus said, "No one knows, however, when that day or hour will come—neither the angels in heaven, nor the Son; only the Father knows. Be on watch, be alert, for you do not know when the time will come." Mark 13:32-33 (From the Gospel for the First Sunday in Advent)

The World

An alarm clock, a telephone, the sound of a phone ringing on a cassette tape.

We want to listen for two ringing sounds today. First, the sound of an alarm clock. The alarm clock rings to tell us to get up and go to school. You can make the clock ring at whatever time you want. See—you just turn this button on the back so the alarm hand is at the time you want it to ring. When that time comes the alarm will sound. (Let it ring.) An alarm clock never surprises us because we tell it when to ring.

Today we want to say that celebrating Christmas is like waiting for an alarm clock to ring. We say that Jesus was born on December 25th. Even though we are not sure about the exact day, we are sure He was born. So we pick a day and get ready for it. We have ___ days until Christmas. It will not surprise us. We will get ready. When the day arrives, we will rejoice because God loves us and has sent His Son to be our Savior.

Now let's listen for another ringing sound. The telephone also rings. It calls us to talk to friends who may want to see us or may want us to come and see them, who may have something important to say, or who may just want to visit for a while. We can't decide when our phone will ring. The person who does the calling makes that decision. Sometimes people who are expecting a call will sit for hours and wait for it to ring. At other times the phone will ring, but no one will answer because the call wasn't expected.

If the alarm clock can remind us to get ready for our celebration of Christ's first coming to earth, the telephone can remind us to be ready for His second coming. In our Bible reading Jesus says He will come to earth again. He also tells us that we will not know what day or what hour He will get here. He will call us. We can't make the phone ring, but we can wait for it. So also we can't make Him come, but we can wait for Him.

Jesus wants us to be ready for His coming. We celebrate Christmas, the first time He came, so we will be ready for His second coming. As you prepare for Christmas this year, listen to all the Old Testament promises that God made. He told us many times, He would send a Savior. When Jesus came, the promises were all kept.

And Jesus made some new promises. Our Bible reading is one of the new promises. It is a promise that He will come to get us and will take us home with Him. That's why we are glad about His second coming. We are happy that He is coming to judge us because first He came to save us.

So we are to live every day waiting for His call. (Push the button on the cassette to sound the telephone.) That's the phone ringing now. Do you think it is Jesus calling? Some day it will be. When Jesus does return, He won't have to use a telephone to let us know He is here. But when the phone rings at your house, imagine that it is Jesus calling. And remember He calls you because He loves you.

How Near Do You Live to Advent Road?

The Word

This is the Good News about Jesus Christ, the Son of God. It began as the prophet Isaiah had written: "God said, 'I will send My messenger ahead of You to open the way for You.' Someone is shouting in the desert, 'Get the road ready for the Lord; make a straight path for Him to travel.'" Mark 1:1-3 (From the Gospel for the Second Sunday in Advent)

The World

A large map of an isolated area. (Either a road map of an isolated area or draw a map showing few cities and roads.) A marker pen.

Let's pretend you own ten acres of land in the middle of this desert (show on map). The land is not worth much because no roads are near it. You can't even drive out to see your own land.

Then you learn that a new road is going to be built through the area. It will be called Advent Road. That's a good name for a road because Advent means coming. The new road means people can come to all of this area where they could not travel before. (Draw a heavy line through the area. Label it Advent Road.) The road will change the area. People can now build homes and businesses beside it. If the road is near your land, your land will become more valuable.

Today's Bible reading pictures us living in a desert like this. And it tells how Old Testament prophets promised to build an Advent Road to us. One prophet said, "God said, 'I will send My messenger ahead of You to open the way for You.'" Isaiah said, "Get the road ready for the Lord; make a straight path for Him to travel." God wanted to build a road from Himself to His people: so Jesus could come to them. Over 1,900 years ago He sent John the Baptist to prepare the people of that time to have

Jesus come into their lives. John told the people to repent of their sins and to receive the forgiveness that Christ came to bring.

And God still builds His Advent Road today. The road still comes from Him to His people. He wants the road to come to you. He wants His Son to come into your life every day. Ask yourself: How near do you live to Advent Road?

We get ready to celebrate the birth of God's Son on Christmas day by moving to Advent Road. For that road to come near our lives God has to knock down our high hills of selfishness, hatred, and jealousy that block God out. He has to fill in the valleys of our spiritual laziness, our fears, and our lack of faith.

But remember: God does not ask us to build the road so His Son can come to us. Because Christ has come, the road is built. Because He died to pay for our sins, the hills that separate us from God are knocked down. Because He came back from the dead, He has filled in the ditches that separate us from God.

Advent Road is already a part of our lives. During this season we want to check the road out, to repair it, and most of all to know that God uses it to come to us daily.

What Do You Want for Christmas?

The Word

God sent His messenger, a man named John, who came to tell people about the light, so that all should hear the message and believe. He himself was not the light; he came to tell about the light. John 1:6-8 (From the Gospel for the Third Sunday in Advent)

The World

A newspaper with several large Christmas ads.

Don't you like to look at the ads in the paper this time of year? You see pictures of toys, games, clothes, and other Christmas gifts. Some children like to look through the ads and play a wishing game. It goes this way: On each page you can pick out one gift that you would like for Christmas. On this page I would like to have this (select another gift).

Of course, I could easily get what I asked for. See. I asked for this (point to the first item); so I can have it. (Tear out the picture and hold it.) And I wanted this (second item). (Tear it out. Keep the two pictures and put the paper down.) I asked for these two things, and now I have them. But you know that I didn't want the pictures from the paper. I wanted the real gifts. The pictures are only reminders that the gifts are in the store. None of us would want to open a Christmas package and find only pictures of gifts.

When John came and preached about the Savior, some people thought he was the Savior. They wanted him to take away their sins. But he told them he was not the light of the world. Instead he was the one who pointed to the light. He wanted to tell them about the Savior so they would go to Jesus and follow Him. John was like an ad in the newspaper. He was not the gift, but he showed others that the gift was available.

Now think about your plans for Christmas this year. What do you want for Christmas? Not just the gifts and the parties, but also the special gift from God. How will you plan to receive again that Baby who has taken away your sin and given you a life that will never end?

Look at all the ways that are offered to you. They are like ads in the newspaper. The special worship services on Christmas Eve and Christmas Day. The Christmas carols. The greeting cards. Special messages about Jesus in magazines and newspapers. Symbols of His birth in a stable will be everywhere.

All of those things are good. But they are only ads in the paper. When you go to the worship services, hear and sing the Christmas carols, read the Christmas cards, you must see the message of Jesus. See His love for you and all people. Understand again that the birth of Jesus is real. God did come to earth to live with us.

What do you want for Christmas? Look at all the ways you can be reminded of the Savior of the world. Then receive the greatest gift of all—Jesus Christ.

A Dream Made Real

The Word

The angel said to Mary: "You will become pregnant and give birth to a son, and you will name Him Jesus. He will be great and be called the Son of the Most High God. The Lord God will make Him a king, as His ancestor David was, and He will be the king of the descendants of Jacob forever; His kingdom will never end. Luke 1:31-33 (From the Gospel for the Fourth Sunday in Advent)

The World

A "Dream Book"—staple together four sheets of paper (large enough so the kid in the back can see). Draw or paste pictures of gifts the children would like on the first three pages. On the last write: "All these gifts given to _____." Another dream book—same except first page says, "Son of the Most High God"; the second, "A King"; and the third, "His kingdom will never end."

Only a few days until Christmas. Many of you are thinking about the gifts you will receive and the gifts you will give. It's fun to look at Christmas ads and dream about what you might get for Christmas. See the dream book I made. It has pictures of some things that many boys and girls would like for Christmas. Here is a bicycle. See the swimming pool—that would be nice next summer. Look at this beautiful dog. What nice gifts to dream about!

But look at the last page. It says, "All these gifts will be given to," then there is a blank for a name. The dream book is really a gift certificate. Someone could fill in your name, and the dream would become real. The gifts would be yours. Wouldn't that be great! Of course, your name isn't filled in the blank; so it is still a dream.

Now let's look at another dream book. This one comes from

the Bible reading for today. The first page says that Jesus is the Son of the Most High God. We talk about God and want to know more about Him. But Jesus knows all about God, because He is God's Son. The next page says He is a King. We've never seen a king. Kings are just people in a book or movie. But Jesus is a king. He is greater than all other kings. It says, "His kingdom will never end." All other kings die and the country gets new rulers. But Jesus will be King forever.

This dream book tells us about Jesus, but sometimes He seems far away. When we hear how great Jesus is, we think He is in a dream book—something we can't really have. But look at the last page. "All these gifts give to," and the blank again. God wants to give His Son Jesus, the King who rules forever, to us.

This time the name is filled in. God said to Mary, "You will become pregnant and give birth to a son." God filled in the blank in the gift certificate. He gave His Son to Mary to be her Son. But God did not just put Mary's name in the blank. He also put in your name and my name. He gave Jesus to everyone. When Jesus became Mary's Son, He also became our Brother. As our Brother, He died for us to remove our sins. Now He wants us to live in His kingdom forever.

16

Grace and Truth in a New Box

The Word

The Word became a human being and, full of grace and truth, lived among us. We saw His glory, the glory which He received as the Father's only Son. John 1:14 (From the Gospel for Christmas Day)

The World

A piece of fine jewelry in a fancy box and a Cracker Jack box.

Look at this beautiful necklace. (Show jewelry in the fancy box.) Maybe you would like to have given something like this to your mother for Christmas. But this gift would be too expensive for most boys and girls to buy. It is the kind of a gift your father may have given your mother.

(Holding the boxes where they cannot be seen, move the necklace from the fancy box to the Cracker Jack box.) Now look at this gift. Here is a necklace. Would you like to give it to your mother? Maybe you thought the other one was too expensive for you. But you might think that anything from a Cracker Jack box was not good enough.

But let me show you something. (Show both containers.) See—I have only one necklace. First you saw it in a fancy box—the one it was sold in. Then I put it in the Cracker Jack box. It looked more valuable in the first box. But it is exactly the same necklace, and its value does not change when it is put in a different box.

Let's use the necklace in the two boxes to understand something about Jesus when He was born on this earth. In our Bible reading Jesus is called "the Word." In the paragraphs before, it says He is God and that He helped create the world. When we see Jesus as God, we can see grace and truth in Him.

Grace is God's love that we do not deserve. Truth is what we can trust, what we can be sure of. We can see grace and truth in God. They are like this necklace in the fancy box (show it). Grace and truth look right with God.

But notice what our Bible reading says, "The Word became a human being, and full of grace and truth, lived among us." Grace and truth are a part of God. But the Bible reading tells us that Jesus became a human being, like us. Yet He was still full of grace and truth. (Move the necklace from the fancy box to the Cracker Jack box.) The same grace and truth that was in God came to be a part of a human being. Jesus brought grace and truth to our lives. No longer is God's grace something so great that we cannot have it. Because Jesus came to earth to be a part of us, God's grace and truth are a part of us also.

The Bible reading says, "We saw His glory, the glory which He received as the Father's only Son." As we celebrated Christmas a few days ago, we saw how Jesus who was God became also a person. Remember Jesus did not give up His grace and truth when He became one of us. Rather He brought that grace and truth to us; so we can share the blessings of His life.

If You Have to Return Your Gift

The Word

The time came for Joseph and Mary to perform the ceremony of purification, as the Law of Moses commanded. So they took the Child to Jerusalem to present Him to the Lord, as it is written in the law of the Lord: "Every first-born male is to be dedicated to the Lord." They also went to offer a sacrifice of a pair of doves or two young pigeons, as required by the law of the Lord. Luke 2:22-24 (From the Gospel for the First Sunday After Christmas)

The World

A model car or other gift that came in a box.

Suppose you got this model car as a Christmas gift. If you liked to build models, this would be a great gift. But what would you think if the person who gave it to you said he had to have it back? The store where he bought the gift told him they had to recall all the model cars. That means you lose your car. Then the person who gave you the gift said the store only had to *account* for each car they sold. So if you would return one end of the box (tear off a section of the box), you could keep the gift. That would be nice. You wouldn't need the box anymore anyway.

When Jesus was born, Jewish parents were also told they had to give their first-born sons back to God. God gave the son to the parents. Then He recalled the gift. He did that to remind the Jews that He had spared their first-born sons at the time of the first Passover. Such was not the case with the Egyptians— they had not put the blood of the lamb on the doorposts.

Instead of giving the son back to God, parents could sacrifice two pigeons. In Egypt a lamb died in place of the first-born son. When Joseph and Mary took Jesus to the temple, they killed two pigeons as a sacrifice so they could keep their son. Just as returning part of the box was a substitute for returning the model car, the pigeons were substitutes for the new baby boy.

As a baby Jesus' life was spared because two pigeons died in His place. Later He became the sacrifice who died in the place of us all. It works this way:

God created us to be good, but we all have sinned. So God had to recall all of us. The recall meant we would lose our lives. Because of our sin, something is wrong with each of us. Our wrong separates us from God.

But God still loves us even though we have sinned. He sent Jesus to earth to be our substitute. Christ died in our place, just as the pigeons died for a first-born Jewish son, or as the box end was returned in place of the model car. When Christ died for us, He took our punishment from us. He died in our place.

So now when we die, our death does not mean we will be separated from God. Instead we can be with God. When God recalled us to Him because we were sinners, it meant we were to be punished. But because Christ has taken the punishment, He now calls us to live with Him forever.

Why Some and Not Others?

The Word

He (Jesus) came to His own country, but His own people did not receive Him. Some, however, did receive Him and believed in Him; so He gave them the right to become God's children. They did not become God's children by natural means, that is, by being born as the children of a human father; God Himself was their Father. John 1:11-13 (From the Gospel for the Second Sunday After Christmas)

The World

Eight dolls, but not babies. Use either the Barbie/GI Joe type doll, make stick figures from Tinker Toys, or cut out child figures from cardboard.

Our Bible reading tells us that some people believed in Jesus when He came to earth and some did not. Still today, some believe and some do not. We often ask why some go to heaven and some go to hell. If everyone is a sinner, it seems all should be lost. But if God loves everyone, and He does, and Christ died for everyone, and He did, it seems everyone should be saved. But Jesus says some will be saved, and some will be lost.

To help understand why this is true, let's hear a story about these eight children (show the dolls) who wanted to join a choir. The choir was good—so good they were going on a four-week trip to Europe.

These four (separate the dolls) tried out for the choir. They studied their music and practiced every day. But they weren't good enough. They didn't make the choir. They didn't go on the trip.

These four knew they couldn't sing very well. But they loved music and wanted to be with the choir on the trip to Europe. They told the choir director they couldn't sing well enough to make the choir, but they still wanted to go. He told them the choir needed someone to carry the instruments and luggage. They offered to do it. So they went on the trip.

Now let's tell the story this way. God has made a place for us to live with Him forever. We want to be in heaven with Him. Some (take the first four dolls) try to get to heaven the natural way. They work hard. They do the best they can. But when they try out for heaven, God tells them they are not good enough. They don't make the trip.

Others know they are not good enough to be in heaven. But they love God and want to be with Him forever. So they ask God, "Can we go, even though we are not good enough?" And God says yes. He finds a way for them to be saved.

That way is Jesus Christ. He came to earth to save us because all of us have sinned and given up our place in heaven. The Bible reading says some people would not receive Him. They couldn't trust anyone else. So they try to save themselves and are lost.

But the reading also says that some did receive Him. They asked Him to save them. And He made them the children of God.

God has come to us. Jesus invites you to be with Him forever. Listen to His invitation. He offers you something you could not earn yourself.

How Long Will You Live?

The Word

A week later, when the time came for the baby to be circumcised, He was named Jesus, the name which the angel had given Him before He had been conceived. Luke 2:21 (From the Gospel for the Name of Jesus)

The World

Three red ribbons, one 12 inches, two 30 inches. A 36-inch white ribbon attached at the middle of one of the 30-inch ribbons. Put all the ribbons in a box and pull one end of each of the red ribbons through a small hole in its lid.

Another year has ended, and another year has started. All of us are growing older. Often we do not understand time. We are eager for some things to happen; so we like time to go by fast. But we want other things to last longer, so we wish time would slow down.

To help understand time, suppose these ribbons are people. The length of the ribbon is the length of a person's life. See, as I pull the ribbons out of the box they appear to be long. An older person has more ribbon showing than a younger. (Make one longer than the others.) We can see how long people have lived by looking at their age.

But we can't see how much longer we have to live. We know how much ribbon is out of the box, but not how much is left in the box. We all know how long we have lived, but none of us know how long we will live. Some people can't enjoy their lives because they are worried about how much time they have left. Some will have short lives. (Pull out the short ribbon.) Others will have long lives. (Pull out the longer ribbon without the white ribbon attached.)

To be able to enjoy our lives, we have to be free from worry about how long we will live. God has taken that worry from us. Today we not only celebrate New Year's Day, but also the naming of Jesus. When He was one week old, Mary and Joseph took Jesus to a rabbi. He was circumcised, and this marked Him as a Jewish person. They named Him Jesus as the angel had told them to do.

Jesus was different from other babies. He didn't have just so many years to live like we do. (Show the ribbons out of the box.) He is also different because He gave His life for us. The name Jesus means Savior. He saved us by giving His life for ours. His life became a part of our lives—like this. (Pull the last red ribbon out so the attached white ribbon shows.) The white ribbon is Jesus. He has connected His life to ours. Because He lives in us, we live in Him. He is a part of our lives, and we are a part of His.

Now we don't have to worry about how much life we have in the box. When our life on earth ends, our life with Jesus will continue. (Pull the red ribbon from the box leaving the white ribbon in the box.) We don't know how long we will live on earth. But we know we will live forever with Jesus.

Know More Than the Right Answer

The Word

He (Herod) called together all the chief priests and the teachers of the Law and asked them, "Where will the Messiah be born?" "In the town of Bethlehem in Judea," they answered. Matthew 2:4-5a (From the Gospel for the Epiphany of Our Lord)

The World

A local phone book.

Today I want to teach you something that you may already know. This is the phone book—the kind that most of you have at home. Did you know about this special page (show it) in the phone book? It has the numbers that you would need in an emergency. Here is the number for the fire department (repeat it), the police, and the ambulance. And here is a place for you to add your doctor's number.

Maybe you already knew about the emergency numbers in the phone book. Most people have seen them at one time or the other. But when an emergency happens, people often forget about this special page. If the house is on fire, or an accident happens, many people don't know how to get help. They know the numbers are there, but they don't use what they know.

I said I wanted to teach you something that you might already know. I do want you to know about the emergency numbers, but that's not what I want to teach you today. Instead I want to help you understand that sometimes we know things that could help us, but we don't use what we know. The phone number is an illustration.

Another illustration comes from our Bible reading for today. It tells us that some men who had studied the stars came to Judea after Jesus was born. They went to King Herod and asked where the new King was born. Herod was upset at the idea of another king. He called together all the chief priests and the teachers of the Law and asked them, "Where will the Messiah be born?" They answered, "In the town of Bethlehem in Judea."

The chief priest and the teachers of the Law knew the right answer from the book. They told the others how to find the Messiah. But they didn't go look for Him for themselves.

We also often know the right answers—from the phone book or the Bible. But sometimes we don't use the answers to help ourselves. If the question is: Will I go to heaven? the answer is; Yes, because Jesus is My Savior and has taken away my sin. We know the answer from the book, but do we always live with the joy and faith that can be ours because we are going to heaven?

If the question is: Why should I try to stop sinning? the answer is: Because God loves me and all people. Sin hurts me and others. God does not want us to be hurt. We know why we should not sin, but do we use what we know?

You can think of other questions that you can answer. But knowing the right answer from the book is not enough. When you use what you know to help yourself and others, you not only know the answer—you also believe the answer.

To Test or to Teach

The Word

Not long afterward Jesus came from Nazareth in the region of Galilee, and was baptized by John in the Jordan. As soon as Jesus came up out of the water, He saw heaven opening and the Spirit coming down on Him like a dove. And He heard a voice from heaven: "You are My own dear Son. I am well pleased with You." Mark 1:9-11 (From the Gospel for the First Sunday After the Epiphany)

The World

On a large poster (Chalkboard or transparency for an overhead projector) write: Sue gave the game to: A: him and I. B: he and I. C: him and me. D: he and me.

Which is the proper ending for this sentence? (Show the poster.) "Sue gave the game to:"—now you pick the answer. You know "he and me" does not sound right. But often children, and even adults, have a tough time knowing which of the other answers is correct.

I could use this sentence to test you. By asking each of you to pick an answer, I would find out how much you know about grammar. Some of you know the right answer. Some of you could guess and be right.

But I can also use this poster to teach you the correct answer. The answer is "C. Sue gave the ball to him and me." We would never say, "Sue gave the ball to he." or, 'Sue gave the ball to I." Instead, we say, "She gave the ball to him; she gave the ball to me." So when we put them together we say, "Sue gave the ball to him and me."

But we are not here to study grammar today. We want to learn something about Jesus. When Jesus came to earth, He became a person who seemed to be like many other people on

27

this earth. Many other people have also become great. Many others have been great teachers. Others have helped people. We have another multiple choice question: Who has done the most for the world? There can be many answers to that question. The Bible reading for today gives us God's answer. When Jesus was baptized, God spoke from heaven and said to Him, "You are My own dear Son. I am well pleased with You."

Other people have done great things. Others have helped us in many ways. But Jesus is the only person who is also the Son of God. Jesus is the only one to whom God could say, "I am well pleased with You."

Jesus did not come to test us. He did not become a person to disguise Himself to see if we could find out who He was. Rather He came to teach us. He came to show us that He is God's Son and also our brother. When He was baptized God told us who Jesus was. In His life Jesus showed us who He was when He showed that He had God's power and wisdom.

Then Jesus gave Himself for us. He took our sin and gave us His goodness. Because He did that, God can say to you, "You are My own dear child. I am well pleased with you."

Jesus was baptized, and you are baptized. In His baptism God taught us that Jesus was His Son. In your baptism God shows you that you are His child too. You are God's because God's Son claimed you.

Plug Into a Plug That's Plugged In

The Word

The next day Jesus decided to go to Galilee. He found Philip and said to him, "Come with Me!" Philip found Nathanael and told him, "We have found the One whom Moses wrote about in the book of the Law and whom the prophets also wrote about. He is Jesus son of Joseph, from Nazareth." John 1:43,45 (From the Gospel for the Second Sunday After Epiphany)

The World

An electrical socket, three extension cords, a lamp that can be plugged into a socket.

Today's Bible reading tells about several events that show us how God worked a long time ago when Jesus lived on earth. We want to use it to see that God still works the same with us today.

See this electrical socket in the wall. Today we will use it as a reminder of Jesus. The socket is like Jesus because it is a source of power. See—when I plug the lamp in, it lights up. Jesus is a source of power. He gives the power to live, the power to love, the power to change our sinful lives to be like His holy life. When we plug into Him, we have a new life.

Our Bible reading tells us that Jesus found Philip and said to him, "Come with Me!" Jesus asked Philip to plug into Him, to receive His power. The lamp could be a reminder of Philip. Instead, let's use this extension cord as a symbol for Philip. See, the extension cord can plug into the socket and carry the power away from the wall. When Philip plugged into Jesus, he carried the power of Jesus with him.

Then Philip found Nathanael and told him, "We have found the One whom Moses wrote about in the book of the Law and whom the prophets also wrote about. He is Jesus son of Joseph, from Nazareth." Philip carried the power from Jesus to Nathanael. See—when I plug the light into this end of the cord, the same power is here as was back at the wall socket.

Later Nathanael also became a disciple. He carried the power of Jesus on to others. (Plug the second extension cord into the first. Show that it works by plugging the light in.) Those who learned about Jesus from Nathanael also carried the power on to others. (Plug in the third cord and show that it works.)

Jesus gave His power to people who gave it to other people. That is how you and I learned that Jesus is our Savior today. But we are not at the end of almost 2,000 years of spiritual extension cords. When we learn about Jesus from other people, we then receive our power directly from Him. (Take the third extension cord back to the wall socket and plug it in.)

Each of us is directly connected to Jesus because He gave His life for us, and the Holy Spirit has called us to Him. At times we need to receive His power from other people. When you need to know Christ loves you, find someone who is plugged into Jesus and plug into that person. At other times you will need to show others the power of Jesus' love. Then you need to be the spiritual extension cord that carries Jesus' power to them.

What Can Jesus Make from You?

The Word

As Jesus walked along the shore of Lake Galilee, He saw two fishermen, Simon and his brother Andrew, catching fish with a net. Jesus said to them, "Come with Me, and I will teach you to catch men." At once they left their nets and went with Him. Mark 1:16-18 (From the Gospel for the Third Sunday After Epiphany)

The World

Several tubes of artist's paint, a brush and a canvas.

Here is an artist's brush, a supply of paint and a canvas. What could you make with these things? About the only thing I could make with them is a mess. (Give an honest evaluation of your artistic ability.) Someone who is studying art might use these things for a homework assignment. An amateur artist could paint a picture for his or her own home. But a talented artist could use these same things to paint a picture that would be worth lots of money and might be hung in a famous art gallery.

The value of what can be made with these items depends on who uses them. Remember that as you listen to the Bible reading: "As Jesus walked along the shore of Lake Galilee, He saw two fishermen, Simon and his brother Andrew, catching fish with a net. Jesus said to them, 'Come with Me, and I will teach you to catch men.' At once they left their nets and went with Him."

Jesus made two fishermen into disciples. These two brothers, Andrew and Simon, who later was called Peter, helped carry the gospel of Christ to many parts of the world. Peter wrote two books that are in our Bibles. These men lived almost 2,000 years ago; yet we still talk about them today.

What made Andrew and Simon become great men? Was it because they had special talent? Or did they happen to be at the right place at the right time? Remember the example of the paint and canvas. The value came not from the material but from the ability of the artist. Andrew and Simon became great not because of something in them, but because of the One who called them to follow Him. Jesus told them to come with Him, and He would teach them to share His message of love with others. He made them great.

Many people call us to follow them today. Others want to teach us how to live and what to do. The value of our lives will depend upon the abilities of those whom we follow. Some want to make us do bad things. Some want to make us rich. Some want to make us successful. But Jesus wants to make us to be like Him. He wants to live with us now and for us to live with Him forever.

We might think that no one could make us that good. But remember who it is that called us to follow Him. It is Jesus, God's Son, who gave His life as a way to remove our weakness and give us His strength. Jesus can make you into someone great, but He *is* great!

The Authority to Do

The Word

Jesus ordered the spirit, "Be quiet, and come out of the man!" The evil spirit shook the man hard, gave a loud scream, and came out of him. The people were all so amazed that they started saying to each other, "What is this? Is it some kind of new teaching? This man has authority to give orders to the evil spirits, and they obey Him!" Mark 1:25-27 (From the Gospel for the Fourth Sunday After Epiphany)

The World

All that is necessary to make a peanut butter sandwich plus a jar opener. Make sure the lid on the peanut butter jar is screwed on tightly.

It's much easier to know what to do than to do it. For example: If you wanted a peanut butter sandwich, you know how to make it. Use the knife to spread the peanut butter on the bread. Simple? But—I have a problem. The lid on the peanut butter jar is stuck. I can't get the jar open. I can talk about making a peanut butter sandwich, but I can't do it. I can tell you how to do it—but I can't show you.

Unless, of course, I have this (show the jar opener). With this I can open the jar and make the sandwich. (Do it.)

We have the same problem with being Christians. We know we should love all people. We should forgive everyone who hurts us. We should listen to God's word and pray regularly. We should help all people in need. We should say only good things about each other. It is easy for us to talk about what we should do. I can tell you that you should do such things. And you can agree with me.

But we have a problem. We don't always do the things we know we should do. In the Bible reading the people knew what the man with the evil spirit needed. He needed to be rid of the bad spirit. They might have said to one another, "Isn't that too bad about that poor guy. He should get rid of that evil spirit." But all the talk did no good.

Then Jesus came. When He told the evil spirit to leave the man, the spirit obeyed Him. The man was healed.

Jesus could do more than talk about the problem. He solved the problem because He had authority. Just as I needed the jar opener to open the jar of peanut butter so I could make the sandwich, Jesus has the authority to do something to help people.

Jesus still has that authority today. And He offers the authority to us. We cannot use His authority to do our will, but we can use His authority to do His will. With His power we can do more than talk about love and forgiveness—we can give love and forgiveness. We can do more than talk about the way to help people—we can help them.

Jesus had that authority to do the things He said because He was God. But since He was also a person, He died for us. He gave Himself for us; so we could share His authority. By His death He gave that authority to us. Because He still lives, we can receive and use His authority now.

Three Steps to Help

The Word

Simon's mother-in-law was sick in bed with a fever, and as soon as Jesus arrived, He was told about her. He went to her, took her by the hand, and helped her up. The fever left her, and she began to wait on them. Mark 1:30-31 (From the Gospel for the Fifth Sunday After Epiphany)

The World

A pair of shoes with laces. Cut the lace on one shoe in several places so it can easily be broken. A new lace.

Have you ever been getting ready for church and had a shoe lace break, like this (pull on the lace that is cut)? Sometimes you can tie a lace back together and make it last for a while. But the problem is that if it is weak in one spot, it may also break in another. See (break the other end). A broken lace is a problem, but it is a problem that can be solved.

In three easy steps the problem of the broken lace is gone. First, you have to ask for help. If you put the shoe back in the closet, the lace will still be broken the next time you want to wear the shoe. There would be no reason to put in a new lace, if you weren't going to wear it. So you ask your mother for help. The second step is that she helps you. She gives you a new lace, and you put it in. But don't forget the third step. After fixing the lace, you must wear the shoe. There would be no reason to put in a new lace, if you weren't going to wear it.

Remember the three steps as we talk about today's Bible story. The story has the same three steps. First, the problem was that Simon (his other name is Peter, one of the 12 disciples) had invited Jesus to his home for dinner. But Simon's mother-in-law was sick. They could have hidden the sick lady by telling her to stay in a back room. Instead, when Jesus arrived, they told Him that the mother-in-law was ill. That was Step 1—Peter asked for help. Jesus went to see the sick woman. He took her by the hand and healed her. That was Step 2. Then she got up and served dinner to her family and guests. That was Step 3.

Now let's think about some of your problems. Some people have problems but never ask for help. They worry and gripe about the problem, but they don't give it to someone who can help. Think about the things that bother you the most. Have you asked for help? Don't skip Step 1.

When you take the problem to Jesus, He will help. That's Step 2. Jesus doesn't always help us exactly the way we want. But He does always give help. When you ask Him for help, remember He is the One who has already given you a new life. Jesus loves you so much He died for you. He has already given you the greatest gift of all—Himself. He will help you; in a way that is best for you.

But don't forget Step 3. After the shoe had a new lace, you wore it. After Peter's mother-in-law was healed, she served dinner. After Jesus helps you, you use His help to help yourself and others. His help removes the problem so you can serve Him and others.

Get the Important Message First

The Word

Then Jesus spoke sternly to him and sent him away at once, after saying to him, "Listen, don't tell anyone about this. But go straight to the priest and let him examine you; then in order to prove to everyone that you are cured, offer the sacrifice that Moses ordered." Mark 1:43-44 (From the Gospel for the Sixth Sunday After Epiphany)

The World

A TV dinner and a dish of home prepared food that is an effort to make or a picture of an elaborate meal from the food section of a paper.

Today's Bible reading is a mystery. Jesus had healed a man who had a bad skin disease. Because people thought the disease could spread to others if they touched it, the man had lived alone for a long time. He was glad to be healed so he could go back to his family and work.

But Jesus told the man, "Listen, don't tell anyone about this. But go straight to the priest and let him examine you; then in order to prove to everyone that you are cured, offer the sacrifice that Moses ordered." Jesus wants us to tell others about His love and power so they can come to Him too. Yet He told this man to keep quiet. Yet the man told everyone that Jesus had healed his skin disorder, and many people came to Jesus to be healed also. We would think Jesus would have been glad because He loves everyone. He wants to help all people. Why did He order the man not to tell others about the miracle?

Maybe we can use this story to understand how Jesus felt. Suppose your mother decided to fix a special Sunday dinner. She worked all day Saturday fixing this (show special dish or picture). But since you also had to eat on Saturday, she gave you this (TV dinner) to eat while she was busy preparing the special Sunday dinner.

Now suppose you went out telling everyone that your mother gave you a special treat—a TV dinner for Saturday lunch. Would your mother be happy? She would not. The TV dinner may taste good. It may be good for you. But your mother worked hard to prepare you a special Sunday dinner. If you were going to tell your friends about a good meal, then she would want you to talk about the Sunday dinner.

Now we can understand the mystery of our Bible reading. Jesus came to earth to die for the man in the story. He suffered many things to pay for the man's sins. He also healed the man's skin disease. The suffering and the death of Jesus was a much greater gift than the healing. If the man wanted to tell how great Jesus is, as he should, he ought to have told that Jesus was the Savior from sin, not just a healer from sickness.

Jesus has done many good things for us. We can tell others that he has helped us in school work, healed our sickness, taken care of us on trips, given us nice weather when we wanted to be outside. But speaking only about those things is like telling everyone about the TV dinner his mother gave him. To show appreciation we must speak about the most important gift given. Jesus has not only given us food, clothing, health, and other good things for now. He has also given us eternal life. Let's tell others about the greatest work Jesus has done.

How to Tell the Real Thing

The Word

Seeing how much faith they had, Jesus said to the paralyzed man, "My son, your sins are forgiven." Some teachers of the Law who were sitting there thought to themselves, "How does He dare talk like this? This is blasphemy! God is the only one who can forgive sins!" Mark 2:5-6 (From the Gospel for the Seventh Sunday After Epiphany)

The World

Play coins (metal washers, tokens, buttons) real coins (the price of a soft drink in a local vending machine) and a soft drink.

Some kids were playing store. They had these buttons which they used for money. They could use play money in their store because the things they bought were not real either.

One of the girls said that she was thirsty, and she was going to use some of her money to buy a soft drink from the vending machine. The others told her not to do it. They warned her it was illegal, that is, against the law, to use play money in a coin machine. They also told her the play money would not work in the machine.

But the girl went to the machine and came back with this drink. Some of the children thought she had broken the law. But others knew that buttons would not work in the machine. They knew the girl had real money (show it). She bought her drink with real money, not buttons. The fact that she had the drink proves it. Buttons won't work in a coin machine.

Jesus also proved that He is really God, not just a pretend God. One day some people brought a paralyzed man to Him. Jesus said to the man, "My son, your sins are forgiven." Some people thought, "How does He dare talk like this? This is blasphemy! God is the only one who can forgive sins!"

But Jesus said, "Is it easier to say to this paralyzed man, 'Your sins are forgiven' or to say, 'Get up, pick up your mat, and walk'? I will prove to you, then, that the Son of Man has authority on earth to forgive sins." Then Jesus told the man to get up and walk. The man did. He was healed.

Just as it would be illegal to use a play coin in a vending machine, it would be blasphemy for a person to claim the power of God. Blasphemy is anything that insults God. We can ask God to do miracles, but we cannot claim the power for ourselves.

Jesus proved that He had the power to forgive sins because He also had the power to make the paralyzed man walk. You cannot see the miracle of forgiven sins; you can only feel it. But you can see that a paralyzed man has been healed when he is able to walk.

You and I need to know today that our forgiveness does not come from a pretend Savior. Our forgiveness is not just a wish or a dream. Forgiveness is real. The miracle that proves it is as real as Jesus' death on the cross and His resurrection from the dead. When He came back to life after having been dead for three days, He showed that He is different than any other pretend Savior. He is the real Savior of the world.

A New Way to Live

The Word

Jesus said, "No one uses a piece of new cloth to patch up an old coat. If he does, the new patch will shrink and tear off some of the old cloth, making an even bigger hole." Mark 2:21 (From the Gospel for the Eighth Sunday After the Epiphany)

The World

A piece of newsprint and two pieces of tagboard (all the same size), a marker pencil, a scissors, tape.

In the story from which today's Bible reading comes, Jesus tells the people they have a new way to live. Because He is our Savior we can get rid of the old ways of guilt, getting even, and selfishness. Instead we can live with forgiveness and love for ourselves and others.

We'll make a poster to remind us of our new way to live. I'll write the message on this poster. (As you write "A New Way to Live" on the newsprint, poke the pencil through the paper.)

Look, I made a hole in the paper. But that's no problem. I can patch the hole with this paper. (Cut a small section from one of the tagboards and tape it over the hole.) Now I can finish the poster. (As you're writing, push hard on the patch so an even larger hole is torn.)

That didn't work. Just like Jesus said, "No one uses a piece of new cloth to patch up an old coat. If he does, the new patch will tear off some of the old cloth, making an even larger hole." Instead of patching the thin paper with the thick, I should have changed posters. (Write the message on the other tagboard.) See the pencil can't push through this paper. Now we have a poster that will last.

By ourselves, we are like this poster (newsprint). We are weak and troubles often come to our lives. When Jesus came to be our Savior, He did not just patch up our lives by giving us little pieces to cover up our weak spots. Instead He gave us a whole new life, like this (the second poster.)

But sometimes we don't want the new life that Jesus gives. Sometimes we want just a little patch to cover up bad spots in our old lives.

We are asking only for a patch when we want forgiveness for some sins that bother us but do not admit that all of our life is sinful and needs to be cleaned by Jesus.

We are using patches in our lives if we pray to God only when we have trouble or worship Him only on Sunday or less.

We are using patches when we share God's love with some people but not with others, because we don't want to love all of the people whom God loves.

Are you using patches in your life? Jesus offers you a new life. He renews that gift each day as He continues to take away our guilt and to give us strength.

When Will You Join the Team?

The Word

Then the three disciples saw Elijah and Moses talking with Jesus. Peter spoke up and said to Jesus: "Teacher, how good it is that we are here! We will make three tents, one for You, one for Moses, and one for Elijah." Mark 9:4-5 (From the Gospel for the Last Sunday After the Epiphany)

The World

Equipment used in a sport popular in your area and a trophy for the same sport.

Many schools have a sports award night. They invite all students who have placed on school teams to dinner. The teams that won sit up front, and they receive a trophy like this as a special honor.

When you see the team getting the trophy, you might think, "I'd like to be on that team." You'd like to share in the honor and fun of being on a winning team. But you can't join a team after they've won the trophy. Team members have to sign up before the first game is played. They must go through hours of practice. (Use the athletic equipment to illustrate the practice.) Then the team must go through the season, sharing the disappointment of losing some games as well as the joy of winning others. Only then are you on the team on awards night.

In the Bible reading Peter saw a winning team. Jesus was the team captain. Moses and Elijah were with Him. Jesus did not look the same as He did at other times. His clothes were shining and white. His face was dazzling. Moses and Elijah shared His beautiful appearance because they were on His team that lived beyond death.

And Peter thought, "I want to be on that team too." He

said, "Teacher, it is a good thing that we are here. We will make three tents, one for You, one for Moses, and one for Elijah. Peter liked that awards banquet. He wanted to stay there forever.

But Jesus ignored Peter's offer to build three tents. Instead He asked Peter to go back to work with Him. Peter had to follow Jesus through the struggle of a difficult season. Peter had to see the pain and guilt of other people. He had to watch the Lord suffer and die. He also shared the joy of Christ's victory over death. Then Peter went out as a member of the team to share with the world the good news of Jesus' love.

Now Peter is on the victor's team. Now he has a place beside Moses and Elijah with Jesus the risen Lord. But Peter joined the team during the season, not just for the victory dinner.

We also want to be a part of the victory dinner for the team that Jesus leads through death to eternal life. We all want to be in heaven with Him. But don't wait until then to join the team. Be a part of the preseason practice as you study and learn God's word. Don't be afraid to face the disappointment of losses and defeats. Jesus is the team captain. He has defeated death. He has a place prepared at the victory dinner.

Are You Ready to Make a Swap?

The Word

"The time has come," He (Jesus) said, "and the Kingdom of God is near! Turn away from your sins and believe the Good News!" Mark 1:15 (From the Gospel for the First Sunday in Lent)

The World

An old sweater that is both dirty and raggy and a new sweater.

If this were your sweater (the old one), what would you do with it? It's not pretty. The yarn is so old and worn that it's not worth repairing. If you tried to wash the sweater, it might shrink and would probably fall to pieces. The sweater isn't worth much, is it?

But you might not want to throw it away. Old clothes are sometimes comfortable. You wouldn't have to worry about tearing this sweater or getting it dirty, because it is already torn and dirty. Besides, if this is the only sweater you have, it is better than none. It would help keep you warm on a chilly day. You'd better keep it.

Unless I offer to swap you this new sweater for the old one. You could give up the old one if you had the new one. Even though you would have to be more careful with the new one, you would enjoy it more. It is prettier and would be warmer too.

In some ways our sins are like the old sweater. We like to keep some of our sins because we are comfortable with them. We like to say bad things about some people because we are comfortable with them. We like to tell lies because it keeps us out of trouble. Sinning is like having one old, dirty sweater. It's the only way we know how to live.

But Jesus says, "The right time has come and the Kingdom of God is near. Turn away from your sin." He says stop sinning. Throw the sin away. But we don't want to. Our sin is our excuse. As long as we have our sin, parents and teacher and friends can't expect us to do what is right. We won't give up our sin.

But Jesus didn't just say to stop sinning. He offers to make a swap with us. He says, "Turn away from your sins and believe the Good News!" He will give you good news to replace your sin. The good news is that He takes the sin. He suffers for it. He dies for it. And He gives us forgiveness and a life that lasts forever.

When you don't want to stop sinning, remember what Jesus offers to trade you for your sin. Instead of having to say bad things about others to make yourself feel good, Jesus will make you good by giving you His goodness. Instead of having to lie to keep yourself out of trouble, Jesus will give you truth that helps you accept responsibility for what you have done and will help you do better the next time.

Lent is a good time for us to listen to what Jesus offers us. He says, "The time has come and the Kingdom of God is near!" Now is the time for us to realize we are sinners and to know what God has done to take away our sin. Remember the swap He offers you: He'll take your sin and give you His life.

How to Gain by Losing

The Word

Jesus said, "For whoever wants to save his own life will lose it; but whoever loses his life for Me and for the Gospel will save it." Mark 8:35 (From the Gospel for the Second Sunday in Lent)

The World

Two ice cubes, a glass, a soft drink, and paper towels.

Jesus says, "For whoever wants to save his own life will lose it; but whoever loses his life for Me and for the Gospel will save it." That sounds simple—until you think about it. What Jesus says is backwards according to our normal way of thinking. Let's think about what He means.

First, an illustration: I have two ice cubes. I want to save the first one. So I wrap it in a paper towel and put it in my pocket. You know what will happen. The cube will melt. My pocket will be wet. Even though I've tried to save the ice cube, I've lost it.

Now the second ice cube. I'll put it in a glass and pour something to drink over it. This cube will also melt. I am losing it too. But it is melting for a purpose. It is making the drink cold. When I take a drink, I am getting something good from the ice cube because I am using it.

Could we say: "For whoever wants to save an ice cube will lose it; but whoever loses an ice cube by using it will save it"?

We are like the ice cubes. Just as the ice cubes melt and are gone, we are going to live so long and die. If we try to save our lives by separating ourselves from others we will lose our lives. We try to save our own lives when we refuse to help others. Think how often we say things like: "I don't care what happens to him." "I don't want to get involved in her problems." "I'll take care of myself and let others do the same."

When we try to save our own lives by not caring about other people, we are like the ice cube wrapped in a paper towel. Our lives just melt away and no one benefits from us. When we try to save our lives we lose them.

But when we give our lives to help others, we are like the ice cube in the glass. As we give our lives, we help others. We can give our lives to others in many ways. We can help people who are lonely, afraid, or sad. We give our lives to others when we take time to speak to people who are shy, visit people who are alone, help people who have trouble in school or the neighborhood. When we help others, we must give away our time, our effort, and our money. But by giving away we gain because what we give becomes a part of other people. Instead of letting our lives just melt away, we give our lives to help others.

We can give our lives to help others because Christ gave His life to help us. When Jesus was on earth, He did not live for Himself. He lived for us. He gave His life to pay for our sins; so we could live for Him. Because He gave His life, He saved ours. Now He asks us to follow Him.

God's Right to Tell You What to Do

The Word

The Jewish authorities came back at Him (Jesus) with a question, "What miracle can You perform to show us that You have the right to do this?" Jesus answered, "Tear down this Temple, and in three days I will build it again." John 2:18-19 (From the Gospel for the Third Sunday in Lent)

The World

Several glass jars and rocks in a paper bag.

Some kids found glass jars like these in an alley. They also found some rocks. So they decided to see how well they could throw rocks. They put the jars down the alley a way and threw the rocks at them. After a couple of tries they were able to hit the jars. (Break the jars in the sack by hitting with the rocks.)

A man heard the sound of breaking glass. He came and told them to stop. The kids asked why they had to do what he said. He was not their parent. He was not a policeman. But the man gave them two reasons why he could tell them to stop breaking the jars. First, the jars were his. They came from his garbage can. Second, he owned the property by the alley. He would have to clean up the broken glass or someone might get hurt. The man had two good reasons; so the kids stopped breaking the jars.

Sometimes we wonder why God has a right to tell us what to do. He tells us not to do things that hurt ourselves or others. He tells us not to lie, call others bad names, or hurt others in any way. We are also to help other people when they need it. We sometimes wonder why God can tell us such things.

One time Jesus told some people who were selling animals in the temple what they were doing wrong. He ordered them to get out. The people asked Him to prove that He had the authority to tell them what to do. Jesus had an answer for them and for us.

He said, "Tear down this Temple, and in three days I will build it again." The people thought He was talking about the building where they had been selling animals. Only later did they realize that He was talking about Himself. He told them that He had a right to tell them what to do because their sin would destroy His body, but in three days He would come back to life.

God has the same reason for telling us not to sin. In the first place we are His. He made us. We belong to Him. But because of our sin we have left Him and gone to the garbage can. Yet He still claims us. When we do wrong, He has to clean up the mess just as the man had to pick up the broken glass. Jesus had to die to clean up the mess of our lives. But He not only died, He also rose again. His resurrection from the dead shows His authority over our sin. The sin did not destroy Him. He took the load of sin; yet He lives.

Now He asks us not to sin—not because He refused to clean up the mess any more. That work is done. But He asks us not to sin because He loves us and we love Him. He wants us to be out of the garbage and back with Him. Instead of our adding to the mess, He asks us to be with Him and help Him clean up the mess.

Believe in Something That Works

The Word

Whoever believes in the Son is not judged; but whoever does not believe has already been judged, because he has not believed in God's own Son. John 3:18 (From the Gospel for the Fourth Sunday in Lent)

The World

A small aquarium filled with water, 3 buttons, a teaspoon, a cork, masking tape.

Believe in Jesus—that's the main message you hear from the Bible and from the church. Today's Bible reading says, "Whoever believes in the Son is not judged; but whoever does not believe has already been judged, because he has not believed in God's own Son." Believing in Jesus is important.

Let's use this aquarium and these buttons to show why believing in Jesus is important. The buttons will stand for people. The water in the aquarium is the judgment we must face when we die. If the button sinks in the water, it fails the judgment and is destroyed by death. If the button floats, it passes the judgment and is not destroyed by death.

The first button thinks, "I can pass the test by myself. I can float. I believe in me." But (drop the button in the water) at the time of death, he discovered he doesn't float. He is destroyed by death. Only he didn't know he couldn't float. He had to wait until it was too late to find out.

People who think they do not need Jesus are like that button. If you ignore the subject of death and judgment, if you think you can take care of yourself, if you count on your own goodness, death will destroy you.

Another button: This one knows he will sink by himself. So

he looks for help. He decides that if he were in a spoon, he would be safe. (Tape the button in the spoon.) Only at the time of death did he discover that the spoon could not float either. (Drop the spoon into the water.) The second button had faith, but he had faith in the wrong thing.

We are acting like the second button if we trust money, health, success or other things of the world to get us through death. The same death that destroys us also destroys all the other things in this life. It is not enough just to have faith. We have to have faith in something that helps us.

The third button knew he would sink by himself. But he knew that corks float. So he trusted in a cork. (Tape the button to the cork.) When the time for judgment came, the button had no worries. He knew corks float, and he knew he was attached to the cork. (Drop the cork in the water.) He was safe.

We are like the last button when we realize we need help and know that Jesus gives help. Jesus is the only person who died and came back to life, never to die again. When we face death, we attach ourselves to Him by believing in Him. His power over death is shared with us. We don't have to be judged at the time of death because He had already paid the price of sin. In Him we will live forever.

We Want to See Jesus

The Word

Jesus answered them, "The hour has now come for the Son of Man to receive great glory." John 12:23 (From the Gospel for the Fifth Sunday in Lent)

The World

Two pictures of Jesus, one showing His suffering and the other His resurrection.

Some tourists from Greece came to Jerusalem to celebrate the Passover the year Jesus was crucified. The visitors heard about Jesus and wanted to meet Him. So they found Philip, one of Jesus' disciples, and said, "Sir, we want to see Jesus."

Think how many people have made the same request in the 1,900 years since the events in our Bible reading happened. When we want to see Jesus, we have to look through the pages of the Bible to see how He lived then and how He promised to live with us now. But for Philip the request was easy. He took Andrew with him and found Jesus. He might have said, "Hey, some Greek guys want to see you." Jesus answered, "The hour has now come for the Son of Man to receive great glory."

Philip and Andrew must have thought that Jesus hadn't heard them. Jesus' reply doesn't seem to answer what they asked. But Jesus had heard His disciples correctly. He was saying that if the Greeks stayed in Jerusalem through the Passover they would not only see Jesus, but they would see Him be given great glory. They would see this part of Jesus' life (show picture of suffering). They would see Jesus arrested, beaten, ridiculed, crucified, and buried. They had asked only to meet Jesus so they could tell their friends they had seen Him. But they were there to see Him die for the sins of the world.

We might think that they saw the worst part of Jesus' life. But Jesus says they were there when He was given great glory. We can understand the glory of Jesus the following week when He rose from the dead (show picture of the resurrection). But to see the glory in the resurrection of Jesus from the dead, we must also be able to see the glory in His suffering and death.

When Jesus said, "The hour has now come for the Son of Man to receive great glory," He was talking about the glory of this (picture of suffering). We see the glory of Jesus in His suffering because it shows how much He loves us. We see the glory of Jesus in His pain because it shows that He willingly gave Himself as a holy sacrifice for sinful people. Jesus' greatest glory, one of the things that makes Him different than all other people who have ever or will ever live, is that He could give His life to save all people.

We are like the Greek tourists. We want to see Jesus. We need to see Him both as He suffered and as He won the victory over death. When we have suffering, when we feel pain and sorrow, we need to remember that Jesus shares in that suffering.

And because Jesus shares our suffering, we will also share His resurrection. When we see Jesus, we see a Savior—a Savior who shares His glory with us.

What Can You Use to Praise Jesus?

The Word

Jesus said, "Go to the village there ahead of you. As soon as you get there, you will find a colt tied up that has never been ridden. Untie it and bring it here. And if someone asks you why are you doing that, tell him that the Master needs it and will send it back here at once." Mark 11:2-3 (From the Gospel for Palm Sunday)

The World

Coins, offering plate, an Easter basket.

On the first Palm Sunday many people in Jerusalem stood along the streets and when they saw Jesus they shouted, "Praise God! God bless Him who comes in the name of the Lord!" We also praise Jesus today. As we retell the story we see Him going to the cross to die for our sins. And we say, "Praise God! God bless Him who comes in the name of the Lord."

But one man in the crowd did more than use words to praise Jesus. We don't know the man's name. But earlier that day he had come home and found two strangers untying his colt. At first he must have thought they were stealing the young donkey. But one of them said, "The Master needs it and will send it back here at once." Then the man recognized the two as Jesus' disciples. He let them take the colt. When the man stood in the crowd praising Jesus, he saw the Savor riding on his colt.

Like the people in Jerusalem we use our voices and our words to praise Jesus today. And we can also be like the man who loaned Jesus his colt. We can use what we own to praise Jesus. Think of some of the things you own that you can add to your voice and your words as you thank God that Jesus is your Savior.

First of all think of your money. When you put your gift to God in the offering plate, you are not paying the church. Your money is not to buy a ticket to get into church. Instead the money is a gift. The money joins your voice in saying, "Thank you God, for sending Jesus to be our Savior. We praise You for loving us."

Can you think of other things you own that you can use to praise God? You may receive an Easter basket this year. You could share it with a child in the hospital or a person in a retirement home. When you use what you own to make other people happy, you are praising God; because God also loves the others and wants them to be happy too.

You can also use your smile, your kind words, your politeness, your deeds of love, to praise God. And, of course, you can also use your words. You can join in singing the Palm Sunday songs and prayers that thank God for His love.

Think of your words and your actions together. Say your thanks to God with your voice and show it in the way you use what God has given you.

The End of a Story? Or a Beginning?

The Word

"Don't be alarmed," he (an angel) said. "I know you are looking for Jesus of Nazareth, who was crucified (nailed to the cross). He is not here—He has been raised! Look, here is the place where they placed Him." Mark 16:6 (From the Gospel for Easter Day)

The World

A dozen strips of paper (large enough to be seen in the last pew) of various colors including black and white. Tape

Today we are going to make a paper chain that tells the life of Jesus. This piece (green) will be the birth of Jesus. (Tape it into a loop.) This one will be His baptism. (Loop it through the first to form a chain). This one will be all the miracles that Jesus did. Another link will be for all the parables He told. This one (red) will tell how Jesus was betrayed, arrested, and crucified. Then the black one will tell us He died.

Stories about people generally end with death. But the Bible reading for today says we need another link in the chain that tells the life of Jesus. When friends of Jesus came to His grave an angel said, "I know you are looking for Jesus of Nazareth, who was crucified (nailed to the cross). He is not here—He has been raised." We must add another link (white) to the chain.

The chain is complete. It could be used to tell the story of Jesus. Now let's make a chain for your life. You also were born; so we'll use green to show your birth. You were baptized; so we add another link. This link can remind us that you went to school. As you grow older, you may add another link to show you are married and have children. And another to show what kind of work you will do. Then some day the last link showing death will have to be added.

Death always seems like the last chapter in our lives. Then we remember: Jesus said, "Because I live, you will live also." When Jesus won His victory over death by coming back to life, He not only added another chapter to His life, but also to ours. When He rose from the dead, He promised that when we die we too can come back to life. We can add the resurrection of Jesus to our own lives.

The question is: Do you add the resurrection of Jesus to the end of your life? Or to the beginning? At first though it seems our resurrection belongs at the end—as the victory over death. After we die we will be raised.

But we don't have to wait until we die to enjoy the resurrection. We know it now. We believe it now. The resurrection of Jesus is the beginning of our lives—not the end. (Put a white link through the green one of the second chain.) Because we have a new and eternal life from Jesus our whole lives are changed. He comes to us in our baptism. He is a part of our school work. He is a member of our family. He is with us at work. And when we die, He takes us to heaven.

Today we celebrate because Christ is already with us. Because He lives after He was dead, we will never be separated from Him.

Peace Be with You

The Word

It was late that Sunday evening, and the disciples were gathered together behind locked doors, because they were afraid of the Jewish authorities. Then Jesus came and stood among them. "Peace be with you," He said. John 20:19 (From the Gospel for the Second Sunday of Easter)

The World

The Sunday comics. Three large posters with messages written in balloons as in the comics. "Peace be with you" with an arrow pointing down. "I'm scared" and "Everything is okay" with dots pointing down to show what a person is thinking.

In the funny papers (show comics) you can read what people say and also what they think. Words in a balloon with dots, like this ("I'm scared"), shows what a person thinks. Words with an arrow, like this ("peace . . .), shows what a person says.

This message ("I'm scared") was over the disciples' heads on the first Easter night long ago. Even though they had seen the empy tomb, some of them had talked to angels, all of them had heard Mary say she saw the risen Lord. Even though one of them had seen Jesus; they were all afraid. They all remembered what had happened three days before when Jesus was arrested and killed. They all remembered that the soldiers had tried to grab them too. You know what they were thinking even without this sign over their heads.

If we had balloons over our heads that show what was on our minds, this would often be the message: "I'm scared." We are scared that people won't like us. We are afraid we might not do well in school or a game. We are afraid someone will find out something we did that was wrong. We are scared our parents will get sick, move, or get a divorce. Even though we might not show it to others, we are often afraid.

But as the disciples sat in that locked room Jesus came to them. He said, "Peace be with you." (Show sign.) When the disciples saw Jesus alive and well, their fear was gone. All the pain of the cross and the death of the tomb were gone. He was alive. Their fear was also gone. Instead they thought, "Everything is okay!" (Hold the sign over your head.)

We have celebrated Easter again this year so you and I can also be reminded that Jesus is still alive and with us. When we are afraid (hold the sign, "I'm scared," overhead), we need to hear the voice of Jesus say, "Peace be with you." (Show second sign.) That peace that Jesus gives you comes from the one who died for you and who still lives. The peace He gives is a victory over sin and death.

Then you can think. "Everything is okay!" (Hold up the sign.) Everything is okay because Jesus had made things okay, and He is with you. Remember these three posters in this order. First, "I'm scared." We are all afraid sometimes. Then remember that Jesus says, "Peace be with you." Then you can think, "Everything is okay!"

Learn the Future from the Past

The Word

Then He (Jesus) opened their minds to understand the Scriptures, and said to them, "This is what is written: the Messiah must suffer and rise from death three days later, and in His name the message about repentance and the forgiveness of sins must be preached to all nations, beginning at Jerusalem." Luke 24:45-47 (From the Gospel for the Third Sunday of Easter)

The World

A large poster with the numbers 2, 4, 6, 8, 10 written in a single line. Cover each number with a piece of paper.

Each piece of paper on this poster has a number written under it. Do you know what the numbers are? Of course, you could guess and you might be right. But knowing and guessing are not the same thing.

I'll show you the middle number. See. Let's call that the present. Now let's look at the numbers that come before it. They are the past. So the first three numbers are 2, 4, and 6. Now do you know what the other two numbers are? If they follow the same pattern, they will be 8 and 10. And they do follow the pattern. The last two numbers are like the future. If you know the pattern of the past and the present, you can understand the future.

Let's cover the numbers again to see how Jesus taught His disciples about the future. On the first Easter the disciples doubted that Jesus arose from the dead. But after they were with Him for a while they believed. They understood the present. (Remove the cover from 6.) Then Jesus said to remember the past. He reminded them the Scripture said that He must suffer and would rise from death on the third day.

(Remove cover from 2 and 4.) When the disciples understood the past and the present, they could see the pattern. Jesus told their future. They would go out and preach the message of repentance and forgiveness of sins to the world. Because in the past the Scripture said that God would send a Savior, and because He had come in their time, they could know that in the future they would share that message (remove cover 8 and 10).

Let's cover the numbers one more time to learn something about our future. First we know our present situation (uncover 6). We are baptized in the name of Christ. God speaks to us from the Scripture, and we speak to Him in prayer.

We can also look to the past. First we see how God sent His Son to die for us and to come back to life to give all people a new life. (Remove cover from 2.) We also see how God has continued to share the message of Christ and His forgiveness for 1,900 years. (Remove cover from 4.)

But looking at the past and the present, we can see the pattern of God's way of loving us. So we can also know about the future. We also are to share the message of repentance and forgiveness with other people. (Remove cover from 8.) Because God has loved us so much, we will want to share His love with others. We also can see in the pattern that when we die we will be raised to life again and will be with God forever. (Remove cover from 10.)

We don't have to guess about our future. We can know how God will take care of us in the future because we have seen what He has done in the past and is doing in the present.

You Must Stay in Touch

The Word

Jesus said, "I am the vine, and you are the branches. Whoever remains in Me, and I in him, will bear fruit; for you can do nothing without Me." John 15:5 (From the Gospel for the Fourth Sunday of Ester)

The World

A lamp with a bulb that works and one that does not.

Would you call this a light? (Show the lamp with bulb.) Or is this the light? (Just the bulb) Or this? (Just the lamp) Of course, the bulb and the lamp must be together to make light—like this. (Turn the light on.) However, if the bulb were burned out (place the other bulb in the lamp), the light would make no light. Then the bad bulb would have to be thrown away. But the lamp is still good. Only it needs a new bulb. (Place the other bulb back in the socket.) Now the lamp makes light again.

When Jesus says He is the vine and we are the branches, He gives us a picture like the bulb and lamp. Jesus is the light, and we are the bulbs. The bulbs by themselves can make no light. A bad bulb is like a branch that bears no fruit. It is removed and thrown away. A good bulb makes light because it remains with the source of light—the lamp.

Look at your own life and see in what ways you are like the light bulb that works. The lamp is Jesus. You know He has power. He has power because He is God. He has power to save us because He became one of us. He used His power to fight against sin and death. He has the power of eternal life.

God offers that power to us through Jesus Christ. It's easy to screw the bulb into a lamp to receive its power. But how do you get your power from Jesus. You know that the bulb must

63

touch the lamp to receive electricity. And you must touch Jesus to receive His power. Jesus touched you when you were baptized. Each time you hear the message of Christ's love for you, He touches your life. He touches you as a child when He is with you and your parents. He touches you as a student when He is with you at school. He touches you as a friend when He is with you as you play games and enjoy your friends.

Each time Jesus touches you He gives you power. You receive power to love and forgive. Power to care about other people and to help them. His power is a light for the world. Jesus gives His message of love and His acts of kindness through people who are in touch with Him.

If you know that you are not doing the things that God wants you to do, you have to check to see if you are in touch with Jesus. Don't be afraid of Him. You know He loves you. He forgives you. Be close to Him, and let His power come through you to others.

Remain United with Me

The Word

Jesus said, "Remain united to Me, and I will remain united to you. A branch cannot bear fruit by itself; it can do so only if it remains in the vine. In the same way you cannot bear fruit unless you remain in Me." John 15:4 (From the Gospel for the Fifth Sunday of Easter)

The World

A potted house plant from which you may remove a number of leaves or branches.

I'd like for you to look at two leaves from this plant and see how they are alike and how they are different. (Pinch one leaf off, and hold it next to another that is still on the plant.) First notice how they are alike. (Discuss color, shape, texture, etc. Point out that the two leaves came from the same source.)

Now let's see how they are different. (There may be some differences in size and shape. One may be scarred.) But the greatest difference is that one is still connected to the plant and the other is not. Their past may be the same. But their futures are different. The one that has been removed from the plant will die soon. The other will continue to live.

Jesus tells us that we are all like leaves on a plant. We are alike in many ways. God created all of us. We were all born. We all have bodies and souls. We all share the experience of being people.

Each of us is also different from the others. We come in different colors, shapes, and sizes. Some have been scarred by sickness or accidents. But the big difference among people is our relationship to God. Some are still connected to God like this leaf is connected to the plant. Others are separated from God like this leaf is separated from the plant.

Because we are all sinners, we should fall off the plant. (Pick off several leaves.) Our sin separates us from God. But Jesus came to bring us back to God. he forgives the sin that separated us from God by paying for it Himself. Because He was once separated from God by death and came back to life, we can be with God again. Jesus tells us, "Remain united to Me, and I will remain united to you. A branch cannot bear fruit by itself; it can do so only if it remains in the vine. In the same way you cannot bear fruit unless you remain in Me."

When we look at our past, we are all alike. We are all sinners. We all deserve to fall from the plant and die. But our future depends on our relationship with Christ. He tells us we do not have to die. Because He died for us we can live. We can receive strength from Him to do His will and live forever.

The big difference between the leaf that has been removed from the plant and the leaf on the plant is that the one still on the plant can continue to receive strength from the plant. By our faith in Christ we can continue to receive God's power for life. We are not on our own. We are connected to Him by His life for us. Accept His invitation: "Remain united to Me."

Who Chose Whom?

The Word

Jesus said, "You did not choose Me; I chose you and appointed you to go and bear much fruit, the kind of fruit that endures." John 15:16a (From the Gospel for the Sixth Sunday of Easter)

The World

A large glass jar with a screw-on lid, several smaller jars, and four or five jars or bottle lids of various sizes.

Let's pretend that this jar (the large one) is God. It is a symbol of God who created us and loves us. The God who sent His Son to be our Savior, to live with us on earth and to give us everlasting life in heaven.

If God is the jar; then we are a lid—because we want to be with Him. (Show a small lid that will not fit the jar.) We want to be on the jar. But look, we have a problem. This lid won't fit the jar. We could solve the problem by choosing a different jar. Let's try this one. Not quite. Here, the lid fits on this jar. Now the lids fit, but we have another problem.

The original jar was a symbol for God who gives us eternal life in heaven. Because we didn't fit in that jar, we changed jars. Often people want to choose another god, one that fits into their lives. To get a god that will match our needs, we may want one that doesn't tell us what to do (show another jar). Or one that does not ask us to worship and serve him (show another jar). When we do that, we are choosing a god to match our needs. We are looking for a god that will fit us.

But listen to what Jesus says, "You did not choose Me; I chose you and appointed you to go and bear much fruit, the kind of fruit that endures."

If God is the jar and we are the lid, we cannot choose a different god that will fit us. Instead God is the one who chooses us to fit Him. God has to make the choice according to who He is. (Put on the lid that fits the large jar.)

If we change gods to fit our needs, we lose what God has to give to us. But God can change us. He chooses us, not because we are perfect and fit Him as this lid fits this jar. Instead he chooses us because He can make us fit Him. Jesus can take away our sins that keep us away from God. He can give us love and joy that make us fit with God.

I can't change all these lids so they will fit this jar. I have to pick the one that already fits. But God can change us. He changes us when He calls us to be His own. He changes us when He cleans us in our baptism. He changes us when He forgives us and when He gives us the will and the power to serve Him.

Remember, you have not found God. God has found you. Don't try to change Him to fit your needs, but know that He changes you.

How to Stick with God

The Word

Jesus said, "Dedicate them to Yourself by means of the truth; Your Word is truth. . . . And for their sake I dedicate Myself to You, in order that they, too, may be truly dedicated to You." John 17:17, 19 (From the Gospel for the Seventh Sunday of Easter)

The World

A picture (not framed) and tape.

Our Bible reading comes from a prayer that Jesus said before He left His disciples. In the prayer Jesus asked His Father to dedicate the disciples to Himself. To dedicate means to have a purpose or to stick to something. If you are dedicated to a friend, you stick with that friend. If you are dedicated to a job or a hobby, you stick with that work or play.

Jesus wants us to be dedicated to God. That means He wants us to stick with God. He wants us to be close to Him now, and He wants us to stay close to Him forever.

To understand how we can be dedicated to God, let's compare this picture to ourselves and the wall to God. I want to put the picture on the wall—and I want it to stay there. But (do it) see—the picture won't stay on the wall. Even if I press it tightly against the wall, it falls when I take my hand away. However, this tape will help. First the tape sticks to the picture. Now the tape also sticks to the wall. And the picture stays on the wall because the tape holds it there.

We are like the picture because we can't make ourselves stick to God. We can't dedicate ourselves to God because we are sinners and are separated from Him. But notice that Jesus didn't tell us to dedicate ourselves to God. Instead, He asks God to dedicate us to Himself. He knows that God will use His truth, that is, His word, to bring and to keep us close to Himself.

In that Word, God tells us that He loves us, and He shows us what it means from Him to love us. First, He tells us how He sent His Son to be our Savior, to pay for our sins. Jesus is like this piece of tape. He is dedicated to us. He sticks to us. He stayed with us even when it was necessary for Him to die for us.

Then Jesus reminds us that He also sticks with God. He says, "For their sake I dedicate Myself to You, in order that they, too, may be truly dedicated to You." Because Jesus sticks to both us and to God, we can stick with God. Because He is dedicated to both God and to us, we are dedicated to God.

Are you dedicated to God? Do you read His word? Worship Him? Obey Him? Serve Him? Love the people whom He loves? Do you stick with God and the life that He gives you? If you answer either "No" or "Sometimes" to these questions, remember the way to be with God. You can't dedicate yourself to God. But you can receive the free gift of love from Jesus Christ who is dedicated to you. And He is also dedicated to God. He will help you stick with God.

Faucet, Pitcher, or Glass

The Word

Jesus said, "Whoever is thirsty should come to Me and drink. As the Scripture says, 'Whoever believes in Me, streams of life-giving water will pour out from his heart.'" John 7:37b-38 (From the Gospel for Pentecost)

The World

A faucet, pitcher, and glass.

Jesus says, "Whoever is thirsty should come to Me and drink." Do you think that means that He runs a lemonade stand and He wants you to buy a drink from Him? No! Jesus is not selling lemonade. Nor is He giving away glasses of cool water on hot, dry days. Though Jesus would care if you were really thirsty. He would want you to have a nice, cool drink.

But He's got something much more important than a drink of water for a thirsty person. He is asking you if your soul is thirsty. Do you feel a dry feeling of guilt that needs to be washed away. Do you feel lonely or helpless and know that you need something to take away those empty feelings? Then Jesus asks you to come to Him. He is like this faucet. (Show it.)

When the faucet is connected to a water system, it provides a rush of refreshing water. Because Jesus is God, He is connected to a source of power and love. He asks us to come to Him so He can wash away our sins. He gives us forgiveness and love just like a faucet gives water. When we receive that refreshing drink from the message of Jesus' love for us, we are no longer lonely or helpless. He is with us—with us to stay.

If Jesus is like the faucet, we might think of ourselves as being like this glass. (Show it.) The water goes from the faucet to the glass. Love and forgiveness goes from Jesus to us. That's a good idea. We need what He has to give.

71

But that wasn't the idea that Jesus had. He does say that we are like glasses to receive the life-giving water from Him. Listen to what our Bible reading says, "Whoever believes in Me, streams of life-giving water will pour out of his heart."

We are not like the glass that receives the water from the faucet. Instead we are like this pitcher. (Show it.) The pitcher receives water from the faucet, then pours it on to others. When we receive the water of life from Jesus, He gives us a new life. He saves us to be with Him in heaven. But He also gives us extra power and love. He gives us enough to pass on to others. When we believe in Jesus, the same message that saves us pours out to others.

Look at your life. Are you like a pitcher that has the love of Christ to share with others? How have you shared Christ's love in the last week? Who have you helped in the way that Christ would give help?

If you are not giving, then you need to receive. If you have nothing to pour out of your pitcher, then you need to go back to the faucet to receive more of Christ's love and forgiveness. And He will give you enough to share with others.

What Do You Mean? Born Again!

The Word

Jesus answered, "I am telling you the truth: no one can see the Kingdom of God unless he is born again." "How can a grown man be born again?" Nicodemus asked. "He certainly cannot enter his mother's womb and be born a second time!" "I am telling you the truth," replied Jesus, "that no one can enter the Kingdom of God unless he is born of water and the Spirit." John 3:3-5 (From the Gospel for the First Sunday After Pentecost)

The World

A jar of instant tea, a glass, water, and a spoon.

When Jesus said that people had to be born again Nicodemus asked, "How can a grown man be born again?" The idea of being born a second time sounded impossible to Nicodemus. And it would be impossible if it meant that a person had to be born again in the same way as the first time. But why should a person be born again the same way as the first time. Unless the second birth is different than the first, there is no reason to be born again.

Jesus was talking about a different kind of birth when He said we must be born again. To understand how a person can be born twice, let's see first that something can be made two times.

See this jar of instant tea. It was made at a factory. I imagine that you could visit the factory where the tea was made. The place might even have a guide to show you how the tea leaves were processed into a liquid, how the liquid was dried and made into a powder. Then the powder was placed in the jar, and the factory had finished it's job. The tea was made.

Now this jar of tea is at your house. You are thirsty; so you say, "I think I'll make some tea." You fill a glass with water, put in some tea, and stir it. You have made tea. But the tea was made a second time. First, it was made as tea in the jar. But you can't drink that. Now it is made as tea in the glass. Now it is ready to drink. (Take a sip.) Now it serves the purpose of tea. If the tea were made only the first time, it would serve no purpose. Only when it is made again, can it be drunk. And that's the purpose of tea.

When we were born the first time, we were already separated from God. So we can't serve our purpose either. But Jesus tells us we can be born again. Our second birth is different. It is being born of the water and the Spirit. The second birth brings us back to God through the life and death of Jesus Christ. It makes it possible for us to be what God made us to be because it removes our sins and gives us that new life in Christ.

Remember that birth is something that happens to you. You were born the first time, not because you wanted to be born, but because your parents wanted you. You were born the second time, not because you wanted it, but because God wants you. And now He has you.

A Good Bible Is a Read Bible

The Word

And Jesus concluded, "The Sabbath was made for the good of men; man was not made for the Sabbath. So the Son of Man is Lord even of the Sabbath." Mark 2:27 (From the Gospel for the Second Sunday After Pentecost)

The World

A paperback Bible that is marked with pencil and shows signs of use; and a new, white, zippered Bible that shows no sign of use.

A Sunday school teacher asked her students to bring their Bibles along to class. One child brought this Bible (the used one). He hadn't read all of it, but he had read some of it many times. He had marked parts that helped him and the parts that he didn't understand. He also took the Bible along on vacation and on one picnic. You can see that his Bible has been used a lot.

Another student brought this Bible (the zippered one). He had received it as a special gift from his grandmother. He kept it in a box. He never let it get dusty, and he never touched it if he had dirty hands. The student who had this Bible was surprised when he saw the other Bible.

"The Bible is God's word," he said. "You should take good care of it."

The other student said, "The Bible takes care of me. I don't take care of it."

Sometimes we forget why God gives us certain gifts. We keep the gift rather than use it. The one student kept his Bible. But the other used his to receive God's message.

When Jesus was on earth, some of the people misused the Sabbath, that is, our Saturday. They followed many rules about the Sabbath. They used the day to show how religious they were. But they didn't come close to God and His people in the way they kept the Sabbath. In fact, they used it as a way to show that others were wrong. Jesus finally told them, "The Sabbath was made for the good of man, man was not made for the Sabbath."

We don't live under Sabbath rules anymore. But sometimes we do mix up other gifts from God. For example, we can mix up the way we use the Bible. Jesus might say to us, "The Bible was written for the good of people; people were not made to keep the Bible."

The Bible is God's word. God uses it to show us we are sinners and to show us how He has solved our problem of sin by sending Jesus to be our Savior. The Bible is God's way of reachng out to us with the love and forgiveness that Jesus has earned for us.

We show how we appreciate the Bible by how we use it. The only good Bible is a Bible that is read.

United We Stand

The Word

Jesus said, "If a country divides itself into groups which fight each other, that country will fall apart. If a family divides itself into groups which fight each other, that family will fall apart." Mark 3:24-25 (From the Gospel for the Third Sunday After Pentecost)

The World

Two pieces, the same size, of thin plywood or heavy cardboard.

Do you think you could make this piece of wood stand up on its edge? (Try it.) The edge is too thin. It won't balance by itself. But I can make the piece of wood stand up. See. (Take the second piece of wood and lean the two together to form an upside-down V.) Now the wood stands up because it has another piece to lean on.

Watch the two pieces of wood as you hear the Bible reading for today. Jesus said, "If a country divides itself into groups which fight each other, that country will fall apart. If a family divides itself into groups which fight each other, that family will fall apart."

You can see how easily these boards could fall down again. If one said, "I want to be here," and the other said, "I want to be there," they could not stand. If one wanted to tilt this way, and the other wanted to tilt that way, they would fall down. Only when they help each other can they stand.

Jesus tells us that our families and our country are like these two boards. We have to depend on one another. If we fight against each other, if we can't agree on where we go and what we do, the family or the country will fall. What Jesus said is also true about your class at school, about our church, and about any other group that you belong to. He wants us to know that we need others and others need us. In our church I can lean on you, and you can lean on me. Then we hold each other up. But if we fight against each other, we not only make the others fall down, but we also fall down.

Part of Jesus' love for us is that He also depends upon us. When He became a person, He was united with us. We can lean on Him. We depend on Him to love us, to forgive us, to give us life now and forever. If we divide ourselves from Him, we lose all the blessings He has earned for us.

And Jesus also leans on us. He depends on us to share His message of love with others. He tells us to take care of sick people and feed hungry people. He tells us to give His forgiveness to others.

Think of the many ways Jesus has blessed you by giving you someone to lean on and someone to lean on you. First and most important, you and Jesus are partners. Then you and your family. You as a part of the church. You as a part of school. Maybe some of you have jobs. If so, you and the person you work for must depend upon each other. In our country we must lean on each other. Jesus gives us a way to receive help from others—and to give help to others.

The Kingdom of God Grows

The Word

"What shall we say the Kingdom of God is like?" asked Jesus. "What parable shall we use to explain it? It is like this. A man takes a mustard seed, the smallest seed in the world, and plants it in the ground. After a while it grows and becomes the biggest of all plants. It puts out such large branches that the birds come and make their nests in its shade." Mark 4:30-32 (From the Gospel for the Fourth Sunday After Pentecost)

The World

A seed and that which grows from it. Suggestions: A watermelon and its seed, a tree near the church or classroom and its seed, a tree seed and a picture of that tree.

Jesus wants us to know about the kingdom of God. He tells us about His kingdom so we will know we are in it now and so we also know what it will be like with Him in heaven.

One of the many things that He tells us about the kingdom of God is that it grows. He says the Kingdom is like a small seed. I have this seed. It is so small you might not be able to see it. It is about the size of _____. That is small.

The important thing about the seed is that it contains life. It can be planted and will grow to produce something big like this. See how small the seed is and see what a big thing will grow from it.

The kingdom of God is like this seed because it starts small and because it grows. The Kingdom starts with a simple message for an individual. God loves you. He has sent His Son to be your Savior, to take away your sin, to give you eternal life. The kingdom of God starts for you as a personal relationship between you and God. He calls you to be His.

Then the kingdom of God grows in you. It grows as your

faith in Christ grows. It grows as you learn more about God's love for you and as you also learn to love God. It grows as you find out that God hears your prayers, forgives your sins, helps you fight temptations.

The kingdom of God also grows beyond you. Your faith in Christ is connected with others who also believe in Him. With other Christians you can worship God and be aware that His love is not just for you but is for all people everywhere. Together with other Christians you can help people who need the love of God which you have received through Jesus. You can talk to people who are lonely, be a friend to the new kid who has no friend, listen to the person who has problems, give to the person who needs food or clothing.

The kingdom of God grows. It grows because God continues to work in you and through you. He plants the seed of faith, but He does not leave you once you know Him as your Lord and Savior. He continues to give you the power of the new life in Christ so the Kingdom can grow.

Who Controls the Power?

The Word

Jesus stood up and commanded the wind, "Be quiet!" and He said to the waves, "Be still!" The wind died down, and there was a great calm. Then Jesus said to His disciples, "Why are you frightened? Do you still have no faith?" But they were terribly afraid and began to say to one another, "Who is this man? Even the wind and the waves obey him!" Mark 4:39-41 (From the Gospel for the Fifth Sunday After Pentecost)

The World

An electric light and radio with their cords running to the speaker and an extension cord providing a source of electricity.

Lamp, turn on. (As you speak, plug the light into the extension cord.) Radio, play. (As you speak, plug the radio in.) Lamp, turn off. (Unplug it.) Light, turn off. (Unplug it.)

Can you talk to the light and the radio and make them obey you? If anyone wants to try, they may. You saw me do it. Maybe you know how I did it. See—I hold the plugs for both the light and the radio. I can tell them to turn off or on because I control the source of power. You can't command the light or radio, because you don't have the plugs that control the power.

In our Bible reading Jesus talks to the wind and the waves. He and the disciples were on a boat in a storm. The disciples were afraid and asked Jesus to help them. He stood up and said to the wind, "Be quiet!" And the wind was quiet. He said to the waves, "Be still!" And the waves were still.

The disciples had been afraid of the storm. After Jesus stopped the storm, they were afraid of Him. They said, "Who is this man? Even the wind and the waves obey him!" They were glad He saved them from the storm. But they did not know how He could do it. They saw His great power and were afraid.

81

Jesus was able to tell the wind and waves what to do because He controls the power that moves them. Just as I have the plugs in my hand that control the light and radio, He controls the wind and waves. The disciples knew that if He could turn the wind and the waves off, He could also turn them on. That's why they were afraid.

But Jesus asked them. "Why are you frightened? Do you still have no faith?" He had to teach them more about Himself. He not only had control of the wind and waves, but He also had control of love and forgiveness. He holds the plugs that give us peace and joy. Because He died to remove our sins and rose from the dead to give us a new life, He can turn on that new life in us.

We can ask Jesus to help us because He is God and controls the power. But don't be afraid of His power. His power includes love, joy, and peace. Ask Him to use that power in your life too.

He Gives More than You Ask

The Word

She (a woman who had suffered terribly from severe bleeding for twelve years) had heard about Jesus; so she came in the crowd behind Him, saying to herself, "If I just touch His clothes, I will get well." She touched His cloak, and her bleeding stopped at once; and she had the feeling inside herself that she was healed of her trouble. Mark 5:27-28 (From the Gospel for the Sixth Sunday After Pentecost)

The World

A ball of string (hidden on the speaker's person with about 18 inches of the string exposed through a button hole or threaded through the clothing by a darning needle) and a scissors.

Have you ever needed a piece of string when you couldn't find any. Sometimes you need just a little piece of string, but you need it right now. And there's no string anywhere.

But look—here's some string sticking to my clothes. That's just enough to help. (Pull out the string and cut off 18 inches but leave that amount still hanging.) When you use this string you might need some more. But don't worry—here's another string. (Continue to pull out and cut off several pieces of string.) When you found that little piece of string, you thought you had found enough to take care of your needs. But you really found a lot more. See—here's a whole ball of string. It is enough to last you for a long time.

Something like that happened to a woman who was sick and needed help from Jesus. She had been ill for 12 years, and she thought the only thing she needed was good health. She knew Jesus could heal her. But she didn't want to ask for His help. Instead she decided just to touch the edge of His clothing.

Jesus was in a big crowd of people. She shoved her way to be near Him and touched Him. She was healed. She had what she wanted—like that first piece of string that you were looking for. But Jesus turned and asked who had touched Him. She then talked to Jesus. She discovered she had received much more than good health. She received the love of God. She learned that Jesus who had the power to heal sickness also had the power to forgive sins and to give eternal life.

The woman came to Jesus looking for something like this (small piece of string), and she found this (ball of string). You and I also have to go to God for help often. We need to ask Him to help us in school, to protect us from trouble, to help our families, to keep us from having accidents and much more. We often come to Jesus asking for little pieces of help like the little piece of string. And Jesus helps us. But He always wants to give us more than we ask. He also gives us love and peace. He gives us Himself. From Him we receive the new life He has earned for us.

The Gift Is Great, But . . .

The Word

(The people from Jesus' home town said) "When did He get all this? . . . What wisdom is this that has been given Him? How does He perform miracles? Isn't He the carpenter, the son of Mary, and the brother of James, Joseph, Judas, and Simon? Aren't His sisters living here?" And so they rejected Him. Mark 6:2b-3 (From the Gospel for the Seventh Sunday After Pentecost)

The World

A sandwich on a paper plate and a note.

Suppose you came home from playing with your friends and found this on the kitchen table (show the sandwich). The note says, "Here's a snack for you. Love, Mom." You are hungry and this is your favorite sandwich. But before you eat the snack, you notice that it is on a paper plate. There's no pickle with it. And no napkin. What if you said, "That's not fixed the way I like. It should be on a nice plate, with a napkin and a pickle; so I won't eat it."

That seems like a foolish story. No one who is hungry would refuse a lunch because it is on the wrong plate. But our Bible reading tells about some people who did something just that foolish.

Jesus was back in His hometown, Nazareth. He preached a sermon, and the people were amazed at His wisdom. They also saw Him do miracles, and they knew He had God's power. His power and wisdom showed that He was the Messiah, the Savior they had been waiting for.

But the people said, "He's just a carpenter. He has brothers and sisters who are just like us. So He can't be special." Then the Bible says they rejected Him. They would not believe He was the Messiah.

Jesus also has a message for us. He died for our/sins; so we are free from all guilt. God will not punish us for what we have done wrong because Jesus took the punishment. Jesus arose from the dead and tells us that we can also live again after we die. He has promised us a place in heaven with Him forever.

That's a great gift God has given us. But some people find reasons not to accept the gift. Some say, "I don't want to read the Bible to find out that stuff. What if it isn't true? Then I've wasted my time." Others say, "I won't want to go to Sunday school or church to hear that. It is too dull." So they reject the message God has for them. Because they don't like the way it is given, they refuse the gift.

How about you? Do you look for reasons not to believe in Jesus? Do you find excuses for not hearing His Word and doing what He says? Remember the people of Nazareth. Jesus loved them and helped them just as He loves you and wants to help you. But they rejected Him. They used excuses. Instead you can listen to Jesus. You can accept His message and His love. Then Jesus can continue to give you more and more love.

Don't Add to the Message

The Word

(Jesus) called the twelve disciples together and sent them out two by two. He gave them authority over the evil spirits and ordered them, "Don't take anything with you on the trip except a walking stick—no bread, no beggar's bag, no money in your pockets. Wear sandals, but don't carry an extra shirt." Mark 6:7-9 (From the Gospel for the Eighth Sunday After Pentecost)

The World

A rubber or Styrofoam ball, balloons, ribbons tied into bows, pieces of candy wrapped in paper, pins.

Our Bible reading tells us that Jesus sent His disciples out on a trip. You know what we do when we go on a trip. We pack suitcases full of clothes. We check to see if we have enough money, traveler's checks, and credit cards. But listen to what Jesus told His disciples, "Don't take anything with you on the trip except a walking stick—no bread, no beggar's bag, no money in your pockets. Wear sandals, but don't carry an extra shirt."

Jesus isn't telling us that it is wrong to take money and clothes on a trip. But remember the disciples weren't going on a vacation. Jesus was sending them out to tell the Good News of His love for all people. Our Savior wanted the disciples to do only one thing—that was to tell people about His love for them. He didn't want anything else to hide that important message.

We can apply the same message to our lives. Jesus has told us to tell others that He loves them. Let's pretend this ball stands for the Gospel. The ball is the message that Christ died to pay for our sins and that He came back to life to give us a way

87

to live with Him forever. The ball includes the promise that Christ is with us all the time and that He loves us and helps us.

No we are to take the ball out and give it to others. We want them to know about Christ's love too. But sometimes we do things that hide the message we want to share. We might tell someone to come to church because we have fun there. So we add a few things to the message. (Pin the ribbons and balloons to the ball.) Or we tell people if they go to church God will give them what they want. (Pin candy to the ball.) See what happens when we add to the message. We hide the important part. Others can no longer see the message that Christ loves them.

Sure, we can have fun at church. Part of our love for Christ is that we enjoy each other. Yes, God does hear our prayers and help us. But we still have problems. That's why we also need the Gospel of Christ's love in our lives. We have to take off the extra things (do it) and see what Christ has done, is doing, and will do, in our lives. Then we can show that message to others.

Keep the Problem

The Word

When it was getting late, His disciples came to Him and said, "It is already very late, and this is a lonely place. Send the people away, and let them go to the nearby farms and villages in order to buy themselves something to eat." "You yourselves give them something to eat," Jesus answered. Mark 6:35-37 (From the Gospel for the Ninth Sunday After Pentecost)

The World

A radio or a toy operated by batteries.

You might enjoy having this radio—except for one thing. It doesn't work. When I turn it on, nothing happens. If it were yours you might take it to your mother and say, "Throw this away, it doesn't work."

Your mother might say, "Keep the radio. Fix it so it works." But you can't repair a radio. As you talk to your mother, she offers you new batteries. You put them in. Now the radio works. Instead of throwing the radio away you kept it. Now it. works.

One time Jesus' disciples asked Him to get rid of a problem. Five thousand people were following them. The people were hungry. The disciples told Jesus, "Send the people away." That would have solved their problem because they wouldn't have had to see the hungry people. But Jesus told the disciples that they should feed the people.

However, the disciples couldn't invite that many to lunch. They found five loaves of bread and two fish—not enough for their own meal. But Jesus helped the disciples solve the problem. He took their five loaves of bread and the two fish. He blessed the food and fed the 5,000 people. All the people had enough to eat, and food was left over.

When we pray today, we often ask God to take a problem away from us. Sometimes He answers the prayer the way we ask. But sometimes He tells us to keep the problem. When He tells us to keep the problem He also offers to help us. He told the disciples to feed the 5,000 people; but He helped provide the food.

You could have thrown away the radio and had no way to listen to music and programs. But by putting in new batteries, you had a radio that works. God did the same thing when people first sinned. He could have thrown away the world by destroying people. Instead He sent Jesus to give us a new life. Instead of throwing us away, Jesus saved us. Now we are His people again.

When you have problems, ask God to help you. Sometimes He will take the problem away. But many times He will give you a way to solve the problem. He often gives Himself to us in a way that we can live with a problem or we can overcome it. But He doesn't tell us to do it ourselves. He gives us Himself.

Look Who Asks for Your Help

The Word

Another one of His disciples, Andrew, who was Simon Peter's brother, said, "There is a boy here who has five loaves of barley bread and two fish. But they will certainly not be enough for all these people." John 6:8-9 (From the Gospel for the Tenth Sunday After Pentecost)

The World

A picture of a local bank (perhaps from a calendar ad) and a child's bank with coins.

The 12 disciples had a problem. Thousands of people had come for lunch. Can you imagine trying to feed 5,000 people? The disciples knew they needed help. They did what we should do when we have a problem. They went to Jesus and explained the situation. Jesus asked the disciples what they could do to help the 5,000 people. They didn't have enough money to buy food for everyone. But they did find a boy who had his own lunch—five loaves of bread and two fish.

You know how the story turns out. Jesus takes the bread and fish from the boy and blesses it. Then He feeds the 5,000 people. They all had enough to eat, and they collected 12 baskets of leftovers.

Did you ever wonder why Jesus bothered with the boy's few pieces of bread and fish? If He could make that much food out of so little, why did He need the little? An example from today: If you had 5,000 people coming for dinner, you would worry. If the only money you had was in this bank (shake it), you know you couldn't buy enough food. But if the owner of this bank (show the picture) said you could have all the money you wanted, you'd have no problem. In fact, you wouldn't even bother opening this little bank. Why fool around with dimes and quarters when you need thousands of dollars? Especially if the thousands are available.

But Jesus didn't think that way. He could have fed the 5,000 without using the boy's bread and fish. But He asked for the boy's help. Jesus and the boy were hosts for the dinner. Sometimes we call this story the miracle of the five loaves and two fish. But we should call it the miracle of a little boy and Jesus. They shared together and a miracle happened.

Jesus still works the same way today—and miracles still happen. Though His power and love are like this bank and our power and love are like this kid's bank, He still lets us work with Him. He asks us to be His partners.

Jesus asks us to help Him save the world. He died to pay for everyone's sins and rose to give us all a new life that lasts forever. And He asks us to tell others. We can receive His forgiveness and share it by forgiving others. We have His love; so we can love others.

He asks us to be His partners in many other ways too. He gives us food and asks us to share with others. He gives us time and abilities and asks us to use them to help others.

We may wonder why Jesus doesn't do everything Himself. He could do a better job. But He loves us. He wants to work with us. He wants us to share in His joy of loving others.

Plan for a Life That Lasts

The Word

Jesus said, "Do not work for food that spoils; instead, work for the food that lasts for eternal life. This is the food which the Son of Man will give you, because God, the Father, has put His mark of approval on Him." John 6:27 (From the Gospel for the Eleventh Sunday After Pentecost)

The World

A sandwich and a credit card.

When you are hungry, you want something to eat. You don't want a promise of something to eat later. Suppose you asked for food and I gave you a choice. You could have this sandwich. Or you could have this credit card. Which would you take?

Of course, the sandwich is food. The credit card isn't. You couldn't eat this plastic card. So for hunger, you should take the sandwich. But before you decided, you'd better think about it.

First of all, if you eat the sandwich now, you'll be hungry again in a few hours. Even if the sandwich were big enough to eat some now and keep some for later, it would soon spoil. Then you'd have nothing to eat.

On the other hand you could use the credit card to buy food. You could get what you needed today—and tomorrow and next week. The food wouldn't spoil because you could get what you needed each day. But you have to depend on the credit card. You have to trust that whoever's name is on it will pay your bill. If the card is no good, you'll have nothing to eat but a piece of plastic.

Before you decide listen to what Jesus has to say. "Do not work for food that spoils; instead, work for the food that lasts for eternal life. This is the food which the Son of Man will give you, because God, the Father, has put His mark of approval on Him."

Jesus says we should forget the sandwich. Reach for something that lasts. Of course He is not talking about food and credit cards. But He is telling us how to plan our lives.

Often we have two choices. We must choose what we want right now and what is better for our total life. It is easy to choose what we want now because we think about today's needs first. But sometimes what we want for now hurts us later. Or at least it does us no good later. Instead we should pick those things which will last—the things that help us both now and later. Jesus is not talking about insurance policies, investments, or houses. Those things will last only as long as we live on earth.

But Jesus wants us to have a life that lasts forever. Sure, God wants us to have the food and other things we need for today and as long as we live on earth. But He wants us to have more than that. He tells us to live on His credit card, to depend on Him for a life that will never end. Jesus tells you that you can trust in Him because God the Father has put His mark of approval on Him. That mark of approval is the resurrection from the dead. Jesus died and rose again to give us eternal life.

Plan your life knowing that you will live forever. Don't let the problems of today destroy your hope for the future. Don't let the joys of today make you forget that even greater joys await you in heaven.

Look at Both Sides

The Word

Jesus answered, "Stop grumbling among yourselves. No one can come to Me unless the Father who sent Me draws him to Me; and I will raise him to life on the last day. The prophets wrote, 'Everyone will be taught by God.' Anyone who hears the Father and learns from Him comes to Me." John 6:43-45 (From the Gospel for the Twelfth Sunday After Pentecost)

The World

A large poster with the words "This Way" and an arrow pointing left on one side and the same words with an arrow pointing right on the other.

Suppose you ordered a sign made to point the way to that door. When the sign arrived, you put it up. But look . . . (Show the side that points the wrong way.) You wanted to direct people toward the door, but this arrow points the wrong way. You could turn the sign upside down. (Do it.) Then the arrow is right, but the words can't be read.

You might complain to the person who painted the sign. But the sign-maker would tell you the sign is correct. See. (Turn the sign over.) It is made to point either way.

Some people who listened to Jesus grumbled about what He said. He had told them He was the Bread of Life. They thought He was like the sign—that He pointed the wrong way. They wanted Him to show them the way of God. Instead He showed them the way to Himself. They didn't like that.

But Jesus told them to stop grumbling. He reminded them that the prophets told them, "Everyone will be taught by God." The people knew they had not always listened to God when He taught them. God seemed too holy, too far away, too difficult to understand.

But Jesus came as a person—like the people He was teaching. When He pointed toward Himself, as He often did, He was pointing to something they could see and understand. As the people got to know Him, they discovered He was God also. Jesus is like this sign. Because He is a human being, He points to us—He is the way God came to us. Because He is God, He also points to our Father in heaven. He is the way we go to God. He tells us, "No one can come to Me unless the Father who sent Me draws him to Me." And, "Anyone who hears the Father and learns from Him comes to Me."

Sometimes we also grumble if we see only half of Jesus. If we see Him only as God, we grumble that He is far away, and we can't understand Him. If we see Him only as a person, we grumble that He has no power to help us. But if we look at both sides of Jesus we have no reason to grumble. Jesus points us to Himself; so He can point us to God.

When we see Jesus as a person, we know He has shared in our lives. He is a part of us. When we see Him as God, we know that what He has done has power to save us forever. He tells you that when you believe in Him He will raise you up on the last day.

Eat Your Cake and Have It Too

The Word

Jesus said, "I am the living bread that came down from heaven. If anyone eats this bread, he will live forever. The bread that I will give him is My flesh, which I give so that the world may live." John 6:51 (From the Gospel for the Thirteenth Sunday After Pentecost)

The World

Two decorated cupcakes, each on a serving plate.

Have you ever heard anyone say, "You can't eat your cake and have it too"? Some people want two things when they have to choose one or the other. For example, a student may want good grades and also want to watch TV or play instead of studying. Or you might want to save your allowance for a vacation but also want to spend it for treats this week. In either case someone might say, "You can't eat your cake and have it too."

Here are two cupcakes. See how pretty they are. I'll give one to Sherry and one to Will. Will, you look at yours and think how good it will taste. So you eat it.

Sherry, you look at yours and think how pretty it is. You want to show it to your friends. You want to think how nice it will be to eat it sometime; so you keep yours.

Will and Sherry each had a choice to make. He ate his cake. She kept hers. Will has already enjoyed his cake. Sherry wants to enjoy hers later.

In our Bible reading for today Jesus calls Himself bread not cake. People in His day didn't eat cake. They were glad to have bread. Jesus said, "I am the living bread that came down from heaven. If anyone eats this bread, he will live forever. The bread that I will give him is My flesh, which I give so that the world may live."

Let's compare Jesus as the living bread to the two pieces of cake. Jesus is like bread because we need Him to live. Just as we must have food for our bodies we must also have food for our spiritual lives. Jesus is that food. First, we can say that Jesus is like the cupcake that was on Will's plate. Jesus was here. He lived for us. He gave His life when He died on the cross to pay for our sins. Because Jesus gave His life for us, we can no longer see Him. (Show the empty plate.) He is like the cupcake that was eaten. Jesus' life was taken from Him.

But Jesus is also like this cupcake that we can still see. He gave His life when He died for us. Yet He returned to live with us. He is a living bread. He is with us today.

We do not have to make a choice between a Savior who will die for us and one who will live for us. Jesus does both. In Him, and only in Him, we can have our cake and eat it too. In fact, we cannot choose one or the other. We need to know Him as the Savior who died for us. We also need to know Him as the Savior who lives for us. In Him we find the living bread that gives us life that lasts forever.

Give and Take

The Word

Because of this, many of Jesus' followers turned back and would not go with Him any more. So He asked the twelve disciples, "And you—would you also like to leave?" Simon Peter answered Him, "Lord, to whom would we go? You have the words that give eternal life. And now we believe and know that You are the Holy One who has come from God." John 6:66-69 (From the Gospel for the Fourteenth Sunday After Pentecost)

The World

Six 3 x 5 cards (messages in text below) and a sack of candy.

I've asked Carol to play a game of Put and Take with me. For the game I have this sack of candy and a stack of cards. Carol will take the top card and do what it says. Then the next card and the next. She may quit at any time she wants. Before we start I want to show her what the bottom card says. See, it tells you, "Take all the candy."

Now we start the game. Take the first card and read it. (The cards in order say, "Take five pieces of candy," "Take three pieces of candy." "Give four pieces of candy to a friend." "Put two pieces of candy back in the sack." "Eat one piece of candy." "Take all of the candy." As the child plays the game give her the opportunity to quit after each card. If she considers stopping, remind her of the bottom card which she has seen.)

During the game of Put and Take you gained some and you lost some. But as long as you knew what the bottom card was, you knew that you should continue the game. In some ways being a Christian is like a game of Put and Take. The life of a Christian always starts by God giving the first gifts. First we take. But God also asks us to put. He asks us to use the gifts He has given us. Some people want to quit the game when God asks them to give away what He has given to them. However, we should always remember that God has shown us the last card. It is God's invitation for us to go to heaven with Him.

For example, in today's Bible reading we hear about some people who quit the game before it was over—and some who refused to quit. First, Jesus gave many gifts to a large crowd of 5,000 people. He fed them all they needed to eat. Some had been healed. All heard the message of love and forgiveness. Then Jesus told the people that they must share in His life, that they must eat His body and drink His blood. Many of them didn't like that; so they left Him.

Jesus then asked His disciples, "Would you also like to leave?" Peter remembered the last card. He answered for all the disciples when he said, "Lord, to whom would we go? You have the words that give eternal life. And now we believe and know that You are the Holy One who has come from God."

But we have to answer for ourselves. Think of all the things that God has given to us. Starting with our baptisms, He has given us His love and mercy. Each day He forgives our sins. He also asks us to give—to give love, money, attention, forgiveness to others. Sometimes we are like the people in the Bible reading who did not understand what Jesus was saying. At such times we must always remember the bottom card. Jesus who asks us to give to others is also the One who has eternal life for us. Stay with Him.

Get the Sound and the Picture Together

The Word

Jesus answered them, "How right Isaiah was when he prophesied about you! You are hypocrites, just as he wrote: 'These people, says God, honor Me with their words, but their heart is really far away from Me. It is no use for them to worship Me, because they teach manmade rules as though they were My laws!'" Mark 7:6-7 (From the Gospel for the Fifteenth Sunday After Pentecost)

The World

A portable TV set and a radio.

Jesus had a problem with some of the religious leaders of His day. When He listened to them, He heard them talk about obeying God and reading the Bible. But when Jesus looked at those people, He saw that what they did was not the same as what they said.

You can see the problem this way. (Turn on the TV set so the picture can be seen but the sound not heard. Turn the radio on to a station that is broadcasting something that does not match the picture. Turn the TV to different channels and the radio to different stations and talk about how the pictures and the sound do not go together.)

If you watch the picture on TV and listen to the sound on a radio, you would be confused because the two do not go together. That's how Jesus felt about those religious leaders. He quotes a Bible passage from the Old Testament that describes those people. It says, "These people, says God, honor Me with their words, but their heart is really far away from Me. It is no use for them to worship Me, because they teach manmade rules as though they were My laws."

101

The people wanted to quote God's law, but they wanted others to follow their own laws. Instead of following God, they used God to make others follow them.

We have to look at ourselves and wonder if Jesus would say the same thing about us. First let's list some of our sounds and then look at our pictures.

We talk about forgiveness. We are glad Jesus died to pay for our sins. We pray, "Forgive us our sins, as we forgive those who sin against us." But look at the picture. Do the people who see us, see the joy we have because we are forgiven? Do they see us forgive others?

We talk about love. God has loved us. He sent Jesus to show us that love. Our words say, "We love Him because He first loved us." But do those who see us see that love? Do they see our love for God and His love for others in us?

You can think of other pictures and words that do not match in your life. When you know that what you say and what you do seem like they are coming from different stations, remember why Jesus came to earth. He came to make us complete, to bring what we say and what we do back together. His love and forgiveness changes the part that is on the wrong channel. What He does and what He says become a part of us. Then what we say and what we do come from the same station—because that station is Jesus.

He Does Everything Well

The Word

And all who heard were completely amazed. "How well He does everything!" they exclaimed. "He even causes the deaf to hear and the dumb to speak!" Mark 7:37 (From the Gospel for the Sixteenth Sunday After Pentecost)

The World

A quarter, candy that costs about 25¢ plus a number of other 25¢ items such as a small book, comb, balloons, etc.

Suppose you gave a very young child this quarter and told her she could go to a store and buy this candy. Little children generally like candy. So from that time on when the little girl got a quarter, she would go to the same store and get the same kind of candy.

You might be surprised then to hear her say she didn't like candy anymore. Yet she kept on buying it.

Only after talking to her would you discover her mistaken notion—she felt the only thing she could buy with a quarter was the one kind of candy. Since she used the first quarter to buy candy, she had decided that all quarters were to buy candy. You can imagine how happy the little girl would be to find that with a quarter she could buy balloons, a little book, or other kinds of candy.

Now I am sure that you already know that a quarter can be spent for many things. But do you know that Jesus can also do many things. Some people see the Savior like the little girl saw the quarter. They think He can do only one thing.

For example, most people know that Jesus forgives sins. They are right. He died to pay for our sins. But He does more than just forgive our sins. He also helps us fight against our temptations. He helps us do what is right. He helps us forgive other people who sin against us.

Some people know that Jesus answers our prayers when we are sick. He does help us. But that's not all he does. He also helps us put up with some sickness and other problems. He also helps us learn from the problems we have. Even stays with us when we die and gives us eternal life.

Some people know that Jesus will take us to heaven. That's true, but He is also with us now. He loves us today and is a part of our lives at all times.

We need to see all the things that Jesus can do in our lives. In our Bible reading for today Jesus healed a man who was deaf and unable to speak. The people who saw the miracle realized that Jesus could do more than help those who had a hearing or a speech problem. They said, "How well He does everything!" They remembered His other miracles as well. They listened to His teachings and saw how He loved people. Then they said, "How well He does everything!"

Look in your life and see how Jesus is a part of all you do. Then you will also know that He does everything well.

Guess Who

The Word

On the way He (Jesus) asked them (His disciples), "Tell me, who do people say I am?" "Some say that You are John the Baptist," they answered; "others say that You are Elijah, while others say that You are one of the prophets." "What about you?" He asked them, "Who do you say I am?" Peter answered, "You are the Messiah." Mark 8:27b-29 (From the Gospel for the Seventeenth Sunday After Pentecost)

The World

Three Halloween masks. Popeye, a space man, and a cowboy are used here, but any identifiable masks may be used.

Let's play a game of "Guess who." When I put this mask on, who am I? You see me in the cartoons. That's right. I'm Popeye. And when I put this on, who am I? Now I'm supposed to look like a space man. But with this one I am a cowboy.

Of course, I'm really not Popeye or a spaceman or a cowboy. I'm me—the person you see with no mask.

Jesus asked His disciples to play "Guess who" with Him. He said, "Tell me, who do people say I am?" The disciples said that some people thought Jesus was John the Baptist. Others thought He was Elijah or one of the other Old Testament prophets. The people who gave those answers did not see Jesus. They saw a mask. Of course, Jesus didn't wear the mask. He did not hide His face from the people. But they wore the masks. See, when I put on a mask I can't see as well. The people who wore masks could not see Jesus well. So they did not know who He was.

Then Jesus asked, "Who do you say I am?" Peter answered, "You are the Messiah." Peter saw the real Jesus. Peter knew

God had promised to send a Savior, and he knew that Jesus was that Savior. When Peter saw what Jesus did and heard what Jesus said, he knew who Jesus was.

Who do you think Jesus is? Do you say He is a great teacher? or a good example? or someone who answers prayers? or someone who lived long ago?

Those things are true, but they do not tell us what Jesus really is. If we see Jesus that way, we are wearing masks that keep us from seeing all of Jesus. It's time to take the mask off. See what Jesus has done—and still does. Hear what Jesus has said and still says.

Jesus is God. He is also one of us. He is God's way of reaching out to us. He is our way of reaching back to God.

Our guilt sometimes puts a mask over our face to keep us from seeing all the gifts that Jesus offers us. Our pride makes us think we can save ourselves. Our selfishness makes us look other ways for help. But Jesus will help us take off those masks so we can see Him as He is. Then we will know Him as our Lord and Savior too.

Can You Hear What Jesus Says?

The Word

Jesus said, "The Son of Man will be handed over to men who will kill Him. Three days later, however, He will rise to life." . . . They came to Capernaum, and after going indoors Jesus asked His disciples, "What were you arguing about on the road?" But they would not answer Him, because on the road they had been arguing among themselves about who was the greatest. Mark 9:31, 33-34 (From the Gospel for the Eighteenth Sunday After Pentecost)

The World

Prior to the sermon record the first sentence of the text on a cassette player.

Jesus has something important to say to you in today's Bible reading. Listen to it on this recording. (Play the tape so all can hear.) Jesus said this before He started on His last trip to Jerusalem, where all the things He talked about came true.

But the disciples didn't understand what Jesus was talking about. Later we find out why they didn't understand. The Bible reading says, "Jesus asked His disciples: 'What were you arguing about on the road?' But they would not answer Him, because on the road they had been arguing among themselves about who was the greatest."

Can you imagine how that sounded? Jesus was talking about His death and resurrection. At the same time the disciples were arguing about who was the most important. Let's listen to both at the same time. (Play the tape again and read the part of the text beginning with, "What were you . . .") No wonder the disciples didn't understand what Jesus said. They were talking about themselves rather than listening to the Savior who was offering His life to pay for their sins and promising to rise from the dead so they could live forever.

You and I can have the same problem. Jesus speaks to us to tell us that He died in our place. He tells us that because He lives, we will live also. But often we don't hear Him because we are talking about something else.

Listen: (Replay the tape as you speak) I want a new bicycle. I wish we had a bigger house and a new car. Why don't we go on a long vacation like everyone else?

Think of other things that keep you from hearing Jesus speak to you. Sometimes we say we are too busy. That means we think the other things we are doing are more important than what Jesus has done for us. Even when we are with Jesus, as the disciples were, we think about our own ideas rather than listen to Him.

Now think about how Jesus does speak to you. Listen to what He has to say. If you listen to His message first, you will be able to take care of the other things later.

Don't Mess Up My Faith

The Word

Jesus said, "If anyone should cause one of these little ones to lose his faith in Me, it would be better for that person to have a large millstone tied around his neck and be thrown into the sea." Mark 9:42 (From the Gospel for the Nineteenth Sunday After Pentecost)

The World

A sign: Don't Walk on the Grass. Another sign on a T-shirt (either printed on the shirt or on a paper pinned to the shirt): Don't Mess Up My Faith.

This sign "Don't Walk on the Grass" is a warning. If you walk on the grass, you will kill it. You know that just one step on grass is not going to kill it. But you should also know that if you take the shortcut across grass one time, you will probably do it again. Also if you walk on the grass, others will follow you. The many footsteps will kill the grass. That's why we need signs like this: (show the sign).

In our Bible reading for today Jesus puts a warning sign on us. It says, "Don't Mess Up My Faith." His words were: "If anyone should cause one of these little ones to lose his faith in me, it would be better for that person to have a large millstone tied around his neck and be thrown into the sea." Jesus tells us we are not to destroy the faith of those who believe in Him. He mentions "little ones," and we know Jesus loves children and wants them to follow Him. But He puts this warning sign on all people. We are all children before God.

Notice that the sign does not say, "Leave my faith alone." We need to show concern about each other's faith. Grass must be mowed, and the weeds must be pulled out. But we are not to kill the grass. So also we need to check each other's faith. We need to know what others believe and to share with them what we believe. Our faith grows when we tell others that we believe Christ is our Savior. Our faith also grows when we listen to others tell that they also believe in Jesus.

But the warning sign tells us not to do anything that would hurt another person's faith. We should not laugh at another person's faith. We should not use Jesus' name to curse or swear. We should not make it difficult for someone else to hear God's word or worship Jesus.

Think of ways that other people have hurt your faith. Then remember how your faith is made strong again by hearing the message of Christ's love for you. If you realize you have hurt someone else's faith, ask God to forgive you. Then help that person grow in faith by showing that you know you are forgiven and ready now to offer that same love of Christ to them.

Don't Act Your Age

The Word

Jesus said, "Let the children come to Me, and do not stop them, because the Kingdom of God belongs to such as these. I assure you that whoever does not receive the Kingdom of God like a child will never enter it." Then He took the children in His arms, placed His hands on each of them, and blessed them. Mark 10:14b-16 (From the Gospel for the Twentieth Sunday After Pentecost)

The World

A woman's purse, a man's necktie, a child's stuffed animal.

Sometimes children pretend they are grown up. When a girl carries her mother's purse like this, or a boy puts on his father's necktie like this, they are pretending they are one of their parents. It is fun for children to look ahead to the time when they will be adults.

But today's Bible reading tells adults to look back at the time when they were children. The story tells us that some parents brought their children to see Jesus. But the disciples told the kids to go away. They thought Jesus didn't have time for kids. But Jesus said the disciples were wrong. He loved the children. He said, "Let the children come to Me, and do not stop them, because the Kingdom of God belongs to such as these. I assure you that whoever does not receive the Kingdom of God like a child will never enter it." Then Jesus let the children sit on His lap. He gave them each a hug and a special blessing.

Jesus did not tell adults to pretend they are children. A grown-up could carry a stuffed toy around like this to pretend to be a child. But Jesus told the adults they had to receive the kingdom of God like children.

One of the big differences between adults and children can be seen in the way they receive things. Adults earn the things they receive. They work for their money. They buy their food, clothing, house, and other things. If a friend gives an adult a gift, most grown-ups think they have to give the friend a gift in return that costs just as much.

But children don't think that way. Children are used to having someone give them food, clothing, a place to live, and everything else. A child who receives a gift says thank you and does not try to return a gift of equal value.

Adults have to learn that they are children before God. They do not earn their blessings from God. Instead God gives to them as a father gives to his children. God gave all of us the greatest gift of all—He gave His Son to be our Savior. We cannot give Him any gift to repay Him for that great gift.

Children can help adults understand God's love for us in Christ. Children can accept love from Jesus and enjoy it. They can show adults how to be thankful for such great love.

And as children grow up to become adults, they can remember the importance of always being a child of God. They don't have to act their age by being independent. They can always receive the love and help that Jesus gives.

Don't Let Money Block God's Way

The Word

Jesus said: "It is much harder for a rich man to enter the Kingdom of God than for a camel to go through the eye of a needle." At this the disciples were completely amazed, and asked one another, "Who, then, can be saved?" Jesus looked straight at them and answered, "This is impossible for men, but not for God; everything is possible for God." Mark 10:25-27 (From the Gospel for the Twenty-first Sunday After Pentecost)

The World

A pitcher of colored water, a bottle, a funnel, five one-dollar bills.

We'll use this pitcher of water to learn something about the way God helps us. The water will stand for God's love for us. He loves us so much that He sent His Son to die in our place to remove our sin.

This bottle is us—you and me. And the funnel is the Bible. God uses the Bible to direct His love to us like this: (Put the funnel in the bottle and pour water in). When we hear the message of Christ from the Bible, God's love comes into our lives. Christ is with us, and we will live with Him forever.

But our Bible reading says that money can cause a problem. (Pour water back into the pitcher.) Jesus says, "It is much harder for a rich man to enter the Kingdom of God than for a camel to go through the eye of a needle." Money can be a block between us and God. See: (Roll the dollar bills into a tight roll. Stuff the money into the neck of the funnel from the inside. Put the funnel back in the bottle. Pour water in the funnel.) See— the money is like a cork. It keeps the water from going into the bottle.

Money can also keep us from receiving God's love. If money

becomes too important to us, it will block the way that God gives His love to us. If a person works so hard that he is too tired to go to church, if someone is too busy to read the Bible, if having money or the things money buys is more important than hearing God's word, the money becomes a cork that blocks the way God gives His love.

The disciples were not rich, but they were worried about what the Savior told them. Jesus said, "This is impossible for men, but not for God; everything is possible for God."

Jesus warns us about the dangers of being rich, so we will know that we need His help. All of us have enough money, or want enough money, to have the problems Jesus talks about. We cannot solve the problem ourselves. But God can. He can pull the cork (do it) and let His love come through again.

Look at your life and see if anything is keeping you from receiving the message of God's love. If so, remember it is impossible for you to solve the problem. But God can. He wants to help you. He wants you to know how much He loves you.

The Way to Be Great

The Word

Jesus said, "If one of you wants to be great, he must be the servant of the rest; and if one of you wants to be first, he must be the slave of all. For even the Son of Man did not come to be served; He came to serve and to give His life to redeem many people." Mark 10:43b-45 (From the Gospel for the Twenty-second Sunday After Pentecost)

The World

Four children, each with: 4 pieces of green paper labeled "money"; 4 pieces of red paper labeled "authority"; 4 pieces of blue paper labeled "honor"; and 4 pieces of green paper labeled "responsibility."

These four children are going to help us study our Bible reading today. Each one has the same amount of money. See their money. And they have the same amount of honor, see it, and the same amount of authority and responsibility. The children are all equal.

According to our way of doing things the one who has the most becomes the greatest. Becky, you take two pieces of money from Jim, two pieces of honor from John. Now take one piece of authority and responsibility from each other person. Now Becky has more money, honor, authority, and responsibility than the others. By our standards she is the leader. She's the boss.

But Jesus tells us to look at greatness another way. He says, "If one of you wants to be great, he must be the servant of the rest; and if one of you wants to be first, he must be the slave of all."

Now, Becky, let's try it again following Jesus' advice. Give Jim back his two pieces of money and give him two pieces of your own. Give John his honor back and two extra pieces. Give each other person their authority and responsibility plus a piece of yours. Now Becky has the least. All the others have more than she does. But Jesus says she is now the greatest. She is the greatest because she does not try to take away from others. Instead she wants to give to others. When we take from others, we feel greater because we have more. But we are smaller because we have hurt others. When we give to others we have less, but we are greater because the others appreciate us.

Jesus was a good example for us. He said, "For even the Son of Man did not come to be served, He came to serve and to give His life to redeem many people."

Jesus did not come to take things away from us. Instead He came to give to us. He even gave His own life. He is the greatest of all because He gave Himself for all people. Because Jesus knew He was also God He did not have to take from us to make Himself great. He was great; so He could give.

Because He gave Himself for us, we are great in Him. So we don't have to take from others. We don't have to put others down. Instead we can give to others because we have received so much from Christ.

What Do You Want Me to Do for You?

The Word

"What do you want Me to do for you?" Jesus asked him (Bartimaeus). "Teacher," the blind man answered, "I want to see again." "Go," Jesus told him, "your faith has made you well." At once he was able to see and followed Jesus on the road. Mark 10:51-52 (From the Gospel for the Twenty-third Sunday After Pentecost)

The World

Three brown paper bags filled to give them size and weight.

In our Bible reading Jesus asks a blind man named Bartimaeus a question. Listen to the question and think how you would answer if Jesus asked you the same thing. The question is: "What do you want Me to do for you?"

For a blind man the answer was easy. Bartimaeus said, "Teacher, I want to see again." The blind man wanted to know what his family looked like. He wanted to see his home, his own face in a mirror.

Now, Jesus asks you, "What do you want Me to do for you?" You might have one big need right now. If so your answer is easy. The person I love is sick; make him well again. Forgive me for the wrong I did. Give me something special that I need or want.

Maybe you would want to think about the question a while. You wouldn't want to make a mistake in your answer to such an important question. Would you want to ask for something for now or for later? Think about it.

Make up your mind how you would answer Jesus' question. Now pretend this (a paper bag) is the answer. Maybe what you asked for could not be put in a paper bag, but you can pretend. For the blind man this sack meant that he could see. For someone the sack would mean forgiveness. To another the sack might be a new bike. Pretend that whatever you asked for came in a sack. Jesus handed Bartimaeus this sack and said, "Go, your faith has made you well."

What do you think happened next? Did Bartimaeus—we can't call him the blind man any more—run home to look at his family? Did he go back to see what his home looked like? Or look for a mirror to see his own face? No. The Bible reading says, "At once he was able to see and followed Jesus down the road."

He followed Jesus down the road. Even though Jesus had already given him the one thing he wanted, he still followed Jesus. He knew that anyone who could give him the first sack could also give more (show other sacks). He knew Jesus would again ask him, "What do you want Me to do for you?"

Now think about your answer to Jesus' question. If God gave you what you asked, would you grab the sack and run? Did you ask for something that would draw you closer to Jesus or make you go further away? Sometimes Jesus must say no to our requests because He knows that we would grab the sack and run. But He knew He could heal Bartimaeus—the blind man believed in Him. Jesus had something greater to give Bartimaeus. He also wanted to give Him eternal life. That's what is always in the last sack from our Savior.

When Jesus asks you, "What do you want me to do for you?" you may think also of your needs right now. But when you receive what you asked for, don't grab the gift and run. God has a lot more to give you.

Not Far Away Is Not Near Enough

The Word

(A teacher of the Law said,) "It is more important to obey these two commandments than to offer on the altar animals and other sacrifices to God." Jesus noticed how wise his answer was, and so He told him: "You are not far from the Kingdom of God." Mark 12:33b-34a (From the Gospel for the Twenty-fourth Sunday After Pentecost.)

The World

A maze (as shown) drawn on a large poster or on a transparency for use on an overhead projector.

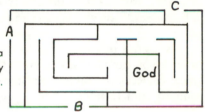

In our Bible reading Jesus and a teacher of the Law talk about the way we are to come close to God. Maybe we can understand their conversation better if we see it on this maze.

The teacher mentioned that some people try to buy their way to God by giving sacrifices. Remember, in those days religious people took a lamb or other animal to the temple to burn as a sacrifice. But the teacher said he had learned that sacrifices were not the way to get close to God. Sacrifice is "A" on this maze. See, by going through "A," I cannot even get close to God. (Mark the possible routes with a heavy line.)

So the teacher said he had found a better way. He said, "It is more important to obey these two commandments than to offer on the altar animals and other sacrifices to God." He is talking about the two commandments that include all of God's law. The two tell us to love God and other people.

Obeying the commandments is "B" on the maze. See (mark

119

the route with a different color or a broken line), if we enter through "B," we can get close to God, but never actually with Him. The Law offers many ways to go, but each one has a dead end that keeps us from God because we can never obey the law perfectly. One sin blocks our way to God.

But Jesus told the teacher, "You are not far from the Kingdom of God." The man had at least learned He couldn't buy a way to be with God. When he also found he couldn't earn God's love, he was close to the real way.

The real way is "C." "C" stands for Christ and the cross. Jesus is the sacrifice that paid for our sins. He obeyed the law that we cannot obey. Therefore, He gives us a new way to come to God. Christ takes us directly to the Father. (Mark the route in bold lines.) The way is clear and easy because Jesus gives it to us.

Just as this teacher talked to Jesus about His way of coming to God, you can also talk to Him. Pray to Jesus and ask for His guidance. Read the Bible to see how God has given you a way to come to Him through Jesus.

How Much Should I Keep?

The Word

(Jesus) called His disciples together and said to them: "I tell you that this poor widow put more in the offering box than all the others. For the others put in what they had to spare of their riches; but she, poor as she is, put in all she had—she gave all she had to live on." Mark 12:43-44 (From the Gospel for the Twenty-fifth Sunday After Pentecost.)

The World

Three coin purses (or coin banks), one with ten dimes, one with five dimes, one with a dime.

"How much should I give?" is a question all Christians have to ask. In Sunday school and in worship service we give offerings. Each of us gives money to help provide a church for ourselves and others and to help other churches. So each one has to answer the question: How much should I give?

Here are three coin purses. We will pretend they belong to three young Christians. This one gives three dimes (take three dimes from the purse with ten and place the three near the purse.) This one gives two dimes (do the same from the purse with five dimes). This one gives one dime (do the same from the final purse).

We can easily see who gave the most and who gave the least. But the Bible reading for today tells us we should look at our giving in another way. It tells how Jesus watched people give money at the temple. Some put in large amounts. A woman put in only two little copper coins. But Jesus said, "I tell you that this poor widow put more in the offering box than all the others. For the others put in what they had to spare of their riches, but she, poor as she is, put in all she had—she gave all she had to live on."

Let's look at the coin purses again. This person (first purse) gave the most, but (show the other dimes) he also kept the most. He gave three and kept seven for himself. This person gave less (second purse). But he also kept less. See, after he gave two dimes, he had only three left. So by Jesus' way of thinking, he gave more than the one who gave three dimes.

Now look at the last purse. This one gave only one dime. Yet, like the widow in the story, he gave all. There is nothing left in the purse. Even though he gave only one dime, he gave more than the others because he gave all he had.

Now look at your own giving. When you ask, "How much should I give?" you must also ask, "How much should I keep?" It is not wrong for you to keep some of your money for yourself. You need food and clothing. You can have and enjoy other gifts from God. But you cannot give God only your leftovers. You should give to Him as He has given to you.

We cannot measure what God has given to us. His greatest gift is not the money we have. The greatest gift from God is His Son who gave Himself as a payment for our sins. Because Christ gave Himself for us, we can give ourselves to Him. Then we can use all that we have as a happy gift from God.

Know What Is Temporary

The Word

As Jesus was leaving the Temple, one of His disciples said, "Look Teacher! What wonderful stones and buildings!" Jesus answered, "You see these great buildings? Not a single stone here will be left in its place; every one of them will be thrown down." Mark 13:1-2 (From the Gospel for the Twenty-sixth Sunday After Pentecost)

The World

Three plates, one paper, one china, one metal (cups may be used).

The advantage of a plate like this (paper) is that it is temporary. You use it once and throw it away. (Crush the plate.) This plate (china) lasts longer. When you use it, you don't throw it away. Instead you wash it and put it back on the shelf to be used again and again. But eventually it too will be thrown away. Someone will drop it and break it, or someone will chip it. This plate is also temporary—only it is temporary for a longer time than the paper plate.

This metal plate can also be washed and reused. It won't break or chip. It will last longer than the other two, but it is also temporary. Eventually it will get bent or lost. Even though it may last a hundred years, some day it will be thrown away.

When we look at many things, we think of them as being permanent—that is that they will always be there. Some houses, bridges, trees, statues and many other things can last a long time—longer than we will live on this earth. To us they seem permanent. One of Jesus' disciples looked at the beautiful temple in Jerusalem. He said, "Look, Teacher! What wonderful stones and buildings!" The disciple thought the beautiful buildings were something worthwhile, something that would really last.

But Jesus said, "You see these great buildings? Not a single stone here will be left in its place; every one of them will be thrown down." Jesus was right. None of those buildings are standing today. They also were temporary.

But what Jesus did was not temporary. He loved people then, and He loves people now. He died to forgive the sins of the people at that time. His death still pays for our sins today. He rose from the dead then. He is still alive today.

Jesus wants us to know what is temporary and what is permanent. Temporary things may last a long time—even longer than we will live on this earth. But Jesus wants us to know that we will also live longer than the 60, 70, or even 100 years that pass between our birth and our death. We will live forever. All other things on the earth are temporary. But because Jesus is our Savior, we are permanent. We will last forever.

Watch for the Signs

The Word

Jesus said, "Let the fig tree teach you a lesson. When its branches become green and tender and it starts putting out leaves, you know that summer is near. In the same way, when you see these things happening, you will know that the time is near, ready to begin." Mark 13:28-29 (From the Gospel for the Twenty-seventh Sunday After Pentecost)

The World

A calendar and a branch from a local tree.

Think how often you look at a calendar like this. You want to know what day it is. Or you want to know how long it is until your birthday or Christmas. Or you look at the calendar to see how many days you have to finish a school assignment or when a ball game is. Calendars are an important part of our lives.

When Jesus lived on earth, the people did not have calendars. But they knew what time of the year it was. They looked at the branches of a fig tree. In our part of the world we would use this kind of tree. We can see the leaves have turned red and brown. They are beginning to fall off. If we didn't have a calendar, this branch would show us that fall is here and winter is coming. Early next spring buds on the tips of the branches will start to grow. That will show us that spring is coming. As the fruit grows, you can tell that spring is turning to summer.

Jesus said that the calendar of a tree should be a lesson for us. Just as we can tell the seasons by the trees, we can also tell about God's plan for us by signs in the world. He says, "In the same way, when you see these things happening, you will know that the time is near, ready to begin."

Our Savior has told us to watch for certain signs. Signs of

war and mistreatment of Christians, signs of strange things in the sky, and signs of false prophets who claim to be the Savior. When those signs appear, they are like the signs of the season on the tree. They tell us something is going to happen. Jesus is going to return to earth to raise the dead and to take those who believe in Him to heaven.

Jesus wants us to know about these signs, so we will be prepared for His coming. The signs do not tell us the hour, day, or even the year when He will come. But they do tell us that He is coming. The signs have been a reminder to each generation that they are to be ready either for their own death when they will go to Jesus or for His final coming when He will come to see them.

We can see the signs of Jesus' final coming in the calendar of history. All of the signs are appearing now as they have appeared before. The signs are God's promises that He has not forgotten us. Jesus came to earth a long time ago to live in our place and be our Savior. He is coming again soon to take us to be with Him. Watch for His signs and be ready for His coming.

Looking for the Right King

The Word

So Pilate asked Him, "Are you a king, then?" Jesus answered, "You say that I am a king. I was born and came into the world for this one purpose, to speak about the truth. Whoever belongs to the truth listens to me." John 18:37 (From the Gospel for the Last Sunday After Pentecost)

The World

An empty saltshaker and a small plastic container filled with salt.

One family always keeps this saltshaker on the table because it matches the pepper shaker. But it has no salt in it. The mother of the family doesn't like to put salt in it because the salt collects moisture. When the salt becomes wet, it won't come out of the shaker. So she keeps the salt in this plastic container. It is sealed; so the salt does not get wet.

Of course the family knows that salt is in this container; so they never use the shaker. But guests will always reach for the saltshaker. They shake and shake and get no salt.

Remember that story and listen to what happened before our Bible reading for today. Jesus had been brought to Pilate for a trial. The enemies of Jesus claimed that He tried to make Himself a king. Jesus did not look like a king to Pilate. The Roman governor thought a king should wear a crown and sit on a throne. He thought a king should have a large army. So Pilate asked Jesus if He were a king.

Jesus had explained that His kingdom was not of this world. A king rules only one country and only for a short period of time. Jesus was not that kind of king. But He was a King. He was King for all countries and for all times.

Jesus did not look like other kings because He was not like

other kings. He didn't need a palace and an army to show that He was a king. He showed that He was a king because He taught the truth. He knew that people were sinful and needed a Savior. He came to be that Savior for all people and to give them a way to live in His kingdom forever.

But people like Pilate did not listen to the truth that Jesus taught. He was like the guests at the table with the empty saltshaker. The guests would reach for what looked like salt. Pilate and all who do not know the truth of Jesus Christ will reach for a king that looks like a king. They will need earthly power and authority.

But at that same table those who knew where the salt really was also knew which container to reach for. Those who listen to Jesus know that He is the real King. Even as He suffered and died, He showed loved, power, and authority far greater than any earthly king. As a king, He does not take from people, but He gives to people. And He says, "Whoever belongs to the truth listens to Me."

Jesus wants you to know He is the real King. Listen to Him. Follow His truth. And tell the others, so they won't have to reach to the wrong king.